**New Directions for
Institutional Research**

Robert K. Toutkoushian
EDITOR-IN-CHIEF

J. Fredericks Volkwein
Paul Umbach
ASSOCIATE EDITORS

# Using NSSE in Institutional Research

Robert M. Gonyea
George D. Kuh
EDITORS

Number 141 • Spring 2009
Jossey-Bass
San Francisco

USING NSSE IN INSTITUTIONAL RESEARCH
*Robert M. Gonyea, George D. Kuh (eds.)*
New Directions for Institutional Research, no. 141
*Robert K. Toutkoushian*, Editor-in-Chief

NEW DIRECTIONS FOR INSTITUTIONAL RESEARCH (ISSN 0271-0579, electronic ISSN 1536-075X) is part of The Jossey-Bass Higher and Adult Education Series and is published quarterly by Wiley Subscription Services, Inc., A Wiley Company, at Jossey-Bass, 989 Market Street, San Francisco, California 94103-1741 (publication number USPS 098-830). Periodicals Postage Paid at San Francisco, California, and at additional mailing offices. POSTMASTER: Send address changes to New Directions for Institutional Research, Jossey-Bass, 989 Market Street, San Francisco, California 94103-1741.

SUBSCRIPTIONS cost $100 for individuals and $249 for institutions, agencies, and libraries in the United States. See order form at end of book.

EDITORIAL CORRESPONDENCE should be sent to Robert K. Toutkoushian, Educational Leadership and Policy Studies, Education 4220, 201 N. Rose Ave., Indiana University, Bloomington, IN 47405.

New Directions for Institutional Research is indexed in *CIJE: Current Index to Journals in Education* (ERIC), *Contents Pages in Education* (T&F), and *Current Abstracts* (EBSCO).

Microfilm copies of issues and chapters are available in 16mm and 35mm, as well as microfiche in 105mm, through University Microfilms, Inc., 300 North Zeeb Road, Ann Arbor, Michigan 48106-1346.

www.josseybass.com

THE ASSOCIATION FOR INSTITUTIONAL RESEARCH was created in 1966 to benefit, assist, and advance research leading to improved understanding, planning, and operation of institutions of higher education. Publication policy is set by its Publications Committee.

# CONTENTS

# Editors' Notes

This volume is about three contemporary trends in American higher education that affect the work of institutional researchers. The first is the unabated appetite for more evidence, accountability, and transparency of student and institutional performance. State and federal governments and other groups continue to demand that colleges and universities demonstrate that they are using their resources in an efficient and effective manner while delivering the best education possible at a reasonable cost (Commission on the Future of Higher Education, 2006). Colleges and universities are expected to assess and evaluate their curricula, programs, and services at all levels to maximize student learning and demonstrate faculty productivity and institutional quality. These circumstances have made additional demands on the time and expertise of institutional research professionals (Howard, 2001; Knight, 2003).

This leads to the second trend: the increased visibility and importance of institutional research offices staffed by highly skilled and competent professionals who can provide campus leaders with objective, trustworthy data about student and institutional performance (Howard, 2001; Terenzini, 1993). Institutional researchers provide evidence for planning, policy formation, and decision making to help an institution more effectively allocate resources in line with its missions, goals, and objectives, thereby demonstrating that the college or university is worthy of the support of its various stakeholders (Saupe, 1981; Dressell, 1981). Toward this end, institutional researchers gather evidence to inform the approval of new academic programs, program reviews, and reports to external bodies such as accreditors. They conduct analyses of existing data that range from the simply descriptive to multivariate modeling to determine what various units are doing and how well. Recently institutional researchers have become more involved in activities to assess institutional conditions that support teaching and student learning outcomes.

The third trend is the ascendance of student engagement and other process indicators that serve as both proxy measures for institutional quality and actionable information to inform improvement efforts. The most widely used of these tools is the National Survey of Student Engagement (NSSE). NSSE's popularity is a function of forces in the external environment that in retrospect all but guaranteed its success, although its developers could not know this at the outset. By the late 1990s, regional accreditors were requiring that all institutions provide evidence of the quality of the undergraduate experience and that institutions use the information they

New Directions for Institutional Research, no. 141, Spring 2009 © Wiley Periodicals, Inc.
Published online in Wiley InterScience (www.interscience.wiley.com) • DOI: 10.1002/ir.282

were gathering to strengthen their programs and practices. NSSE was almost a perfect tool in this regard, inasmuch as it was designed and its reports formatted so that a campus could benchmark its results against those of similar schools and use the data almost immediately to point to places where changes in policies and practices could enhance student engagement. The final report of the Commission on the Future of Higher Education, commonly known as the Spellings Commission, *A Test of Leadership* (2006), recommended NSSE as one of the instruments institutions should use. Subsequently, the Voluntary System of Accountability, a joint effort of the National Association of Land Grant Colleges and Universities and the American Association of State Colleges and Universities, designated NSSE as one of the preferred tools for reporting selected dimensions of the quality of the student experience.

In addition, business leaders and policymakers called for colleges and universities to graduate more students, especially those from historically underserved populations, in order for the United States to remain economically competitive in a global marketplace. Some colleges and universities turned to NSSE because it provided data about activities and institutional actions that decades of research indicated were linked to student persistence and graduation.

Another reason NSSE has been well received is that from the beginning, its staff were unequivocally committed to continuous improvement and working closely with their "customers": institutional researchers and assessment personnel, academic administrators and student life programmers, and leaders of national associations with similar aims. Its National Advisory Board held NSSE staff to high performance expectations, one of which was to make the case to the media for why student engagement mattered to student learning in contrast to institutional resources and reputation, the two major planks on which popular college rankings rested.

As a result, student engagement is now part of the higher education lexicon in North America. This *New Directions for Institutional Research* volume explains the value and relevance of the student engagement construct and how NSSE results have been used for various purposes.

In Chapter One, George Kuh describes in detail the circumstance out of which NSSE emerged, its conceptual roots, and its empirical foundations. He then traces NSSE's development, discusses its mission and guiding policies and practices, and concludes with some observations about how NSSE has influenced the role of institutional researchers.

NSSE was designed to be used by colleges and universities to inform planning, assessment, and improvement. In the second chapter, Trudy Banta, Gary Pike, and Michele Hansen draw on their experiences at different institutions to illustrate how student engagement results can be used toward these ends.

Although NSSE is a fairly short questionnaire, the data can be analyzed in different ways to shed light on aspects of the student experience that are linked to student learning and other dimensions of collegiate quality. In addition, students' responses can be linked to other information an institution has to provide a somewhat nuanced picture of what undergraduates do and what they gain from college. In Chapter Three, Pu-Shih Daniel Chen and colleagues, research analysts familiar with NSSE data, discuss some of the key issues in getting the most out of an institution's student engagement results.

Students do not start college with a clean slate; rather, they come predisposed to engage in certain activities and not others. In Chapter Four, James Cole, Marianne Kennedy, and Michael Ben-Avie describe the Beginning College Survey of Student Engagement and how it can be used to measure entering first-year students' precollege academic and cocurricular experiences, as well as their interest in and expectations for participating in educationally purposeful activities during college. The goal is to better understand the influence of the institution on student performance.

One of the unequivocal findings from the NSSE project is that students generally do what their instructors ask them to do. In Chapter Five, Thomas Nelson Laird and colleagues discuss how faculty members influence student engagement through their teaching methods, priorities for student participation in effective educational practices, and campus leadership. The authors detail four roles faculty can play in assessing student engagement, an approach that can help institutional researchers and others work constructively with faculty members, some of whom tend to dismiss or ignore assessment findings.

In the next chapter, Jillian Kinzie and Barbara Pennipede further illustrate how institutions have used their NSSE results to induce positive changes in teaching, learning, and other institutional practices. Examples from different types of colleges and universities show how faculty, student affairs professionals, academic administrators, and others have worked together to implement policies and practices that foster higher levels of student engagement. They offer six recommendations for how institutional researchers can turn engagement survey results into action.

The founders of NSSE envisioned that eventually student engagement results could be used along with other information to demonstrate institutional effectiveness and respond to public calls for transparency and accountability. In Chapter Seven, Alex McCormick discusses NSSE's contribution toward these ends and how the project has helped shift the national conversation away from institutional resources and reputation as markers of collegiate quality to a focus on what students actually do. McCormick's cogently explicated concept of reflective accountability sits in contrast to notions of external accountability and appeals to the professional sensibilities of educators and institutional leaders committed to quality improvement and public transparency.

Finally, Robert Gonyea and George Kuh use an organizational intelligence framework to tie together the key themes addressed by the authors of the previous chapters. They conclude that effective use of student engagement as an organizing construct for institutional improvement, accountability, and transparency requires that institutional researchers use multiple layers of organizational intelligence (Terenzini, 1993): technical knowledge, analytical skill, and comprehensive understandings about the relevance of engagement the current context.

Taken together, the contributors to this volume make plain why and how student engagement is a concept and data source with which institutional researchers must become familiar and use to help colleges and universities deal productively with the challenges of assessment, improvement, accountability, and transparency.

Robert M. Gonyea
George D. Kuh
Editors

## References

Commission on the Future of Higher Education. *A Test of Leadership: Charting the Future of U.S. Higher Education*. Washington, D.C.: U.S. Department of Education, 2006. Retrieved Sept. 4, 2008, from http://www.ed.gov/about/bdscomm/list/hiedfuture/reports/final-report.pdf.

Dressell, P. L. "The Shaping of Institutional Research and Planning." *Research in Higher Education*, 1981, 14(3), 229–258.

Howard, R. D. (ed.). *Institutional Research: Decision Support in Higher Education*. Tallahassee, Fla.: Association for Institutional Research, 2001.

Knight, W. E. (ed.). *The Primer for Institutional Research*. Tallahassee, Fla.: Association for Institutional Research, 2003.

Saupe, J. L. *The Functions of Institutional Research*. Tallahassee, Fla.: Association for Institutional Research, 1981.

Terenzini, P. "On the Nature of Institutional Research and the Knowledge and Skills It Requires." *Research in Higher Education*, 1993, 34(1), 1–10.

ROBERT M. GONYEA *is associate director of the Center for Postsecondary Research at Indiana University–Bloomington.*

GEORGE D. KUH *is Chancellor's Professor of Higher Education and director of the Center for Postsecondary Research at Indiana University–Bloomington.*

# 1

*This chapter summarizes the history of the engagement concept, the development of the National Survey of Student Engagement (NSSE), and its impact on institutional researchers.*

# The National Survey of Student Engagement: Conceptual and Empirical Foundations

*George D. Kuh*

> Because individual effort and involvement are the critical determinants of college impact, institutions should focus on the ways they can shape their academic, interpersonal, and extracurricular offerings to encourage student engagement.
> —Ernest Pascarella and Patrick Terenzini (2005)

When the history of American higher education is rewritten years from now, one of the storylines of the first decade of the twenty-first century likely will be the emergence of student engagement as an organizing construct for institutional assessment, accountability, and improvement efforts. The engagement premise is straightforward and easily understood: the more students study a subject, the more they know about it, and the more students practice and get feedback from faculty and staff members on their writing and collaborative problem solving, the deeper they come to understand what they are learning and the more adept they become at managing complexity, tolerating ambiguity, and working with people from different backgrounds or with different views. Engaging in a variety of educationally productive activities also builds the foundation of skills and dispositions people need to live a productive, satisfying life after college. Said another way, engagement helps to develop habits of the mind and heart that enlarge their capacity for continuous learning and personal development (Kuh, 2003).

NEW DIRECTIONS FOR INSTITUTIONAL RESEARCH, no. 141, Spring 2009 © Wiley Periodicals, Inc.
Published online in Wiley InterScience (www.interscience.wiley.com) • DOI: 10.1002/ir.283

In this chapter, I briefly summarize the history of the engagement concept and the circumstances that led to development of the National Survey of Student Engagement (NSSE). Then I review the substance and evolution of NSSE and its impact on institutional researchers.

## The Engagement Construct

The engagement premise has been in the literature for more than seventy years, with the meaning of the construct evolving over time (Astin, 1993; Pascarella and Terenzini, 2005; Pace, 1980):

- Time on task (Tyler, 1930s)
- Quality of effort (Pace, 1960–1970s)
- Student involvement (Astin, 1984)
- Social and academic integration (Tinto, 1987, 1993)
- Good practices in undergraduate education (Chickering and Gamson, 1987)
- Outcomes (Pascarella, 1985)
- Student engagement (Kuh, Schuh, Whitt, and Associates, 1991; Kuh and others, 2005)

One of the earliest iterations was the pioneering work of the eminent educational psychologist Ralph Tyler, showing the positive effects of time on task on learning (Merwin, 1969). In the 1970s, drawing on thirty years of his own research, C. Robert Pace developed the College Student Experiences Questionnaire (CSEQ), which was based on what he termed "quality of effort." Pace showed that students gained more from their studies and other aspects of the college experience when they invested more time and energy in educationally purposeful tasks: studying, interacting with their peers and teachers about substantive matters, applying what they are learning to concrete situations and tasks, and so forth (Pace, 1990). Alexander Astin (1984) fleshed out and popularized the quality of effort concept with his "theory of involvement." About the same time, the influential *Involvement in Learning* report (National Institute of Education, 1984), to which Astin was a major contributor, underscored the importance of involvement to student achievement. Since then, scholars such as Ernest Pascarella, Gary Pike, Patrick Terenzini, and Vincent Tinto have contributed scores of papers addressing different dimensions of student effort and time on task and their relationship to various desired outcomes of college (Pascarella and Terenzini, 2005; Pike, 2006; Tinto, 1987, 1993).

Today *engagement* is the term usually used to represent constructs such as quality of effort and involvement in productive learning activities. The introduction and widespread use of the NSSE (Kuh, 2003) and its two-year college counterpart, the Community College Survey of Student Engagement (CCSSE), helped cement student engagement in the higher education lexicon. By design, NSSE and CCSSE demonstrated that student engagement can be reliably measured across large numbers of institutions and that

NEW DIRECTIONS FOR INSTITUTIONAL RESEARCH • DOI: 10.1002/ir

engagement data can be used almost immediately by faculty and staff to improve the undergraduate experience. The growing emphasis on assessment, accountability, and transparency by the Commission on the Future of Higher Education (2006), commonly known as the Spellings Commission, and other groups further highlighted the relevance of engagement as an indicator of student and institutional performance and underscoring the role that institutions have in inducing students to take part in educationally purposeful activities (Kuh, 2001, 2003; Kuh, Schuh, and Whitt, 1991; Kuh and others, 2005). As a result, engagement increasingly has been featured in higher education policy discussions, the scholarly and institutional research literature, and the popular media.

## The NSSE Story Abridged

Since the 1970s, instruments have been available for assessing some aspects of student engagement. These include the CSEQ (Kuh, Vesper, Connolly, and Pace, 1997; Pace, 1990) and a few other national surveys with similar types of questions, such as the Cooperative Institutional Research Program's Entering Student Survey and its follow-up version, the College Senior Survey (Astin, 1993). These instruments, designed and used primarily for research purposes rather than accountability and improvement, were fairly long and cumbersome to administer, which in recent years contributed to lower-than-desired response rates from survey-fatigued undergraduate students.

In the early 1990s, the U.S. Department of Education expressed interest in determining whether tools could be developed to provide institutions with valid, reliable information about the student experience and commissioned an evaluation of existing instruments toward this end (Ewell and Jones, 1996). But as is often the case with government-sponsored work, a change in political winds swept aside concrete steps to pursue the quality improvement agenda.

Even so, others remained convinced of the need for good data to guide improvements in teaching and learning. One such visionary was Russ Edgerton, who left the American Association for Higher Education to direct the education program at The Pew Charitable Trusts, which invested heavily in an educational reform agenda during the late 1990s. In early 1998, Edgerton brought together some experts to discuss ways to shift the national dialogue about collegiate quality from what college rankings typically emphasize—institutional resources and reputation—to authentic evidence of student learning and effective educational practice. Out of that discussion emerged the notion that a valid, reliable, widely used survey of student behavior and experiences could potentially be a helpful, instructive, and useful alternative to rankings. Subsequently Edgerton asked Peter Ewell of the National Center for Higher Education Management Systems to develop an instrument to assess the extent to which students take part in empirically derived good educational practices and what they gain from their college experience (Kuh, 2001).

New Directions for Institutional Research • DOI: 10.1002/ir

Ewell assembled a design team that spent several months developing the prototype of what became NSSE.[1] The main content represents student behaviors highly correlated with many desirable learning and personal development outcomes of college. Most of the items had been used in other long-running, well-regarded college student research programs (for example, the CSEQ and the Cooperative Institutional Research Program). In fact, about two-thirds of the original NSSE items were the same or similar to questions on the CSEQ (Kuh, 2001).

While the survey content was being determined, a handful of institutions and survey research centers were invited to bid on the project. The Indiana University Center for Postsecondary Research (IUCPR) was selected, in large part because of its proposed collaboration with an experienced professional survey organization, the Indiana University Center for Survey Research, and because Bob Pace had transferred the CSEQ to IUCPR in 1994. In 1999, IUCPR staff, in collaboration with the National Center for Higher Education Management Systems (NCHEMS) conducted two field tests, one with twelve schools and a second with sixty-eight institutions, before launching the first NSSE national administration in 2000 with 276 fee-paying colleges and universities.

Pew's hope was that the NSSE project would become self-supporting; indeed, few other efforts have been as successful as NSSE in this regard. Drawing on sound advice from the NSSE National Advisory Board and a Technical Advisory Panel, NSSE used much of The Pew largesse to underwrite the costs of the survey in its first three years to make it very attractive to potential users. The basic cost structure has not changed much since 2003, when Pew support ended and the project became self-sustaining through institutional user fees.

Three factors helped NSSE to hold costs steady. The first was the shift from a mailed paper survey (and its substantial postage and handling costs) to what is now essentially a Web-based survey operation. Second, NSSE enjoyed substantial annual increases in the number of participating institutions (Figure 1.1). Finally, grants and contracts allowed NSSE and its companion surveys at Indiana (Beginning College Survey of Student Engagement, Faculty Survey of Student Engagement, Law School Survey of Student Engagement), all of which also became self-supporting after initial start-up funding, to conduct studies of the psychometrics and use of the instruments, further demonstrating their value in the market.

In the early years, a few institutions, typically small, financially pressed private colleges, blanched at what they considered to be the high cost of NSSE relative to other student surveys. But over time, the versatility and industry-standard customer service provided by NSSE staff proved that the student engagement survey was essentially "institutional research in a box." All an institution had to do was provide NSSE student contact information, and NSSE did the rest, using population sampling for the smallest schools and random samples at larger colleges and universities. Equally important, increasing external pressures by accreditors, state systems, and others to collect and

New Directions for Institutional Research • DOI: 10.1002/ir

**Figure 1.1. NSSE Institutional Participation, 2000–2008**

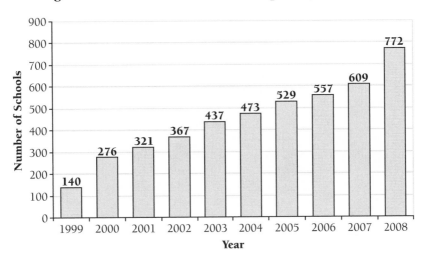

use student experience data for accountability and improvement brought institutions to the realization that they had to spend more than a trivial amount of money on assessment tools for this purpose. In retrospect, NSSE came on the scene just as the "perfect accountability storm" was brewing and was exceptionally well positioned to provide some of what institutions needed with regard to measuring the undergraduate student experience.

## NSSE's Purposes and Philosophy

The NSSE project was founded on and continues to pursue three core purposes. The first, and most important, as represented by the size of the balls in Figure 1.2, is to provide high-quality, actionable data that institutions can use to improve the undergraduate experience. In the absence of actual measures of student learning, student engagement data are "process indicators," or proxies, for learning outcomes. Among the better-known process indicators are the seven "good practices" in undergraduate education, such as setting high expectations and providing prompt feedback (Chickering and Gamson, 1987). Process indicators often point to areas that schools can do something about to improve student and institutional performance (Kuh, 2001; National Survey of Student Engagement, 2002).

NSSE's annual reports and Web site provide scores of examples of how administrators and faculty members are using their NSSE results—such as patterns of student-faculty interaction and the frequency of student participation in other educational practices that they can influence directly and indirectly—to improve student learning. In addition, some states (South

## Figure 1.2. NSSE Core Purposes

Institutional
Improvement

Public
Advocacy

Documenting
Good Practice

Dakota is one of them) and university systems (such as the University of Texas) employ NSSE data in their performance indicator systems and for other accountability functions.

NSSE's second purpose is to discover more about and document effective educational practice in postsecondary settings. It does this in two primary ways: through careful, ongoing analyses of the annual NSSE results including experimental items, and research and related activities undertaken by the NSSE Institute for Effective Educational Practice (see http://nsse.iub.edu/institute/). The NSSE Institute was founded in 2002 to conduct externally funded research and work with institutions and other organizations with goals that complement those of NSSE. A fair amount of institute staff time is devoted to better understanding the factors associated with conditional and compensatory effects of engagement (Pascarella and Terenzini, 2005).[2] NSSE's third purpose is to advocate for public acceptance and use of empirically derived conceptions of collegiate quality. For example, its annual report features the national benchmarks for the five clusters of effective educational practice for different types of institutions. Substantial effort is devoted to making NSSE findings accessible to higher education reporters and the general popular media. NSSE's *A Pocket Guide to Choosing a College: Are You Asking the Right Questions* (2008) encourages prospective students and those who advise them to obtain more instructive information about the institutions they are considering. That is, instead of being satisfied with knowing how many books are in the library, the pocket guide encourages students to find out how many books a typical first-year student there actually reads, how often students discuss ideas outside class with their teachers and peers, and how many students study abroad, have internships, are part of a learning community, or conduct research with a faculty member. Institutions can answer these questions by reviewing their NSSE results.

Several hundred thousand copies of the pocket guide have been distributed nationally over the past few years.

Another of NSSE's advocacy efforts is to encourage institutions to publicly report their performance on NSSE and other indicators of collegiate quality. From the beginning, NSSE officially discouraged the use of student engagement results in any sort of ranking system. Instead we have worked with participating schools, higher education associations, and the media to better understand and focus on what matters to student learning. With NSSE, consumers could learn what they needed to know about the dimensions of student and institutional performance to make informed college choices and to help students maximize their learning and personal development. Today there is widespread agreement that public reporting is long overdue. In 2007, NSSE did its small part to further the transparency agenda by partnering with *USA Today* to make it possible for colleges and universities to post their NSSE benchmark scores and other information on the *USA Today* Web site (http://www.usatoday.com/news/education/2007–11–04-nsse-cover_N.htm).

**Structure of the Instrument.** The NSSE questionnaire collects information in five categories (Figure 1.3). First, it asks students questions about their participation in dozens of educationally purposeful activities, such as interacting with faculty and peers, the amount of time they spend studying or participating in cocurricular or other activities, including work on or off the campus. Seniors report whether they took advantage of such learning opportunities as being part of a learning community, working with a faculty member on a research project, internships, community service, and study abroad. First-year students indicate whether they have done or plan to do

**Figure 1.3. Information Collected in the NSSE Questionnaire**

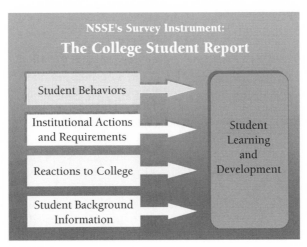

these things. A second set of questions asks students about what the institution requires of them, such as the amount of reading and writing students did during the current school year and the nature of their examinations and coursework.

A third set of questions asks students about their perceptions of features of the college environment that are associated with achievement, satisfaction, and persistence including the extent to which the institution offers the support students need to succeed academically and the quality of relations among various groups on campus such as faculty and students (Astin, 1993; Pascarella and Terenzini, 2005; Tinto, 1993). Students' perceptions are not directly related to how much they learn; however, they are directly related to whether students will persist and are satisfied with their experience and, thus, indirectly related to desired outcomes. Direct measures of student satisfaction are obtained from two questions: "How would you evaluate your entire educational experience at this institution?" and "If you could start over again, would you go to the same institution you are now attending?"

In the fourth category, students provide information about their background, including age, gender, race/ethnicity, living situation, educational status, and major field. Having this information allows NSSE and other researchers to better understand the relationships between student engagement and desired outcomes for different types of students. With campus institutional review board approval, schools have the option to link their students' responses with their own institutional data in order to examine other aspects of the undergraduate experience. Institutions may also compare their students' performance with data from other institutions on a mutually determined basis for purposes of benchmarking and institutional improvement. This greatly enhances the power of student engagement data because institutions can better understand and more accurately estimate the impact of course-taking patterns, major fields, and initiatives such as first-year seminars, learning communities, study abroad, internships, and service-learning on achievement and persistence of students from different backgrounds and majors, as some of the chapter authors of this volume explain later.

Finally, students estimate their educational and personal growth since starting college in the areas of general knowledge; intellectual skills; written and oral communication skills; personal, social, and ethical development; and vocational preparation. These estimates are mindful of a value-added approach to outcomes assessment whereby students make judgments about the progress or gains they have made (Pace, 1984). Although they cannot substitute for direct measures of learning, student self-reported outcomes appear to be generally consistent with other evidence, such as results from achievement tests (Pike, 1995; Pace, 1985).

To make the instrument even more relevant to mission- or context-specific issues, consortia of at least six institutions can add up to twenty additional questions to obtain information specific to the interests of the group. Through 2008, there have been thirty-three groups of institutions that have formed ninety-nine NSSE consortia; some groups, such as Jesuit colleges and women's colleges, have formed consortia multiple times. Twenty-three state or university systems have administered NSSE fifty-five times. (These consortia and systems are listed in Appendix A.)

**NSSE Psychometrics, Benchmarks, and Scalelets.** As with all other surveys, the NSSE relies on self-reports, the validity and credibility of which have been examined extensively (Baird, 1976; Pace, 1985; Pike, 1995). In general, the psychometric properties of NSSE are very good, and individual items and the overall instrument have been tweaked based on data collected over the years from focus groups, cognitive testing, and various psychometric analyses. (Much of this information is available at http://nsse.iub.edu/ pdf/conceptual_framework_2003.pdf.)

To provide a common language and framework for discussing and reporting student engagement and institutional performance results, NSSE at the outset used a combination of empirical and conceptual analyses to identify a small number of clusters, or benchmarks, of effective educational practice (see Appendix B). This was necessary because talking in any comprehensible way about several dozen individual questionnaire items would not encourage instructive, reliable benchmarking against peer institutions or further another important goal of the project, which was to shift the nature of the national conversation about what constitutes quality in undergraduate education. The development of the five benchmarks is explained more fully elsewhere (http://nsse.iub.edu/html/psychometric_framework_2002.cfm).

To increase NSSE's utility, Pike (2006) tested twelve "scalelets," or clusters of questions on similar topics, which often have more explanatory power than the benchmarks. In addition, NSSE adds experimental items every year to see if alternative measures of engagement yield additional insights into what matters to student learning. One such module of items, deep learning, has produced a number of instructive findings that help explain, for example, disciplinary differences in student engagement and self-reported outcomes (Nelson Laird, Shoup, Kuh, and Schwarz, 2008).

## NSSE and the Institutional Research Office

Another reason NSSE flourished is its widespread acceptance by institutional researchers. The NSSE design team was very sensitive to how institutional researchers could use NSSE results and sought input from representatives of the Association for Institutional Research (AIR) in developing the questionnaire and survey administration processes. Toward these ends, NSSE established a technical advisory panel to guide its development in the early years; most of its members were current and former institutional researchers.[3] NSSE staff have been regular contributors to AIR meetings since 2000 and periodically have conducted focus groups with institutional research (IR) personnel there and in other venues. Each year the NSSE reports contain additional information presented in user-friendly formats so that sections of the NSSE institutional report can be duplicated and distributed to various groups on campuses.

Nevertheless, some NSSE practices caused concern among some IR staff. In order to make college and university presidents and senior academic officers aware of the NSSE project, NSSE's National Advisory Board recommended that copies of the institutional and annual reports, along with other periodic correspondence, be sent directly to the president's office with the request to pass on the documents to the IR director and other staff such as the public relations officer. Some IR staff took umbrage at this approach, believing that because they were responsible for collecting and reporting student data for institutional decision making, this information should be delivered to their office first. As NSSE grew in size and influence, some IR directors accustomed to unilaterally determining the assessment instruments used by their school felt pressured by presidents and provosts to use NSSE. As a result, NSSE's intentional efforts to bring student engagement and different conceptions of collegiate quality to the attention of institutional leaders began to change the nature of the relationship between the IR office and senior decision and policy makers.

A salutary side effect of this approach was to increase the visibility and importance of the IR function on many campuses. Presidents more frequently asked IR directors to explain the institution's NSSE results, which prompted more discussions among IR personnel, provosts, academic deans, department chairs, and student affairs professionals. As the NSSE project evolved, NSSE developed mechanisms to alert IR offices in advance as to when NSSE reports would arrive on campus and the key findings would be available electronically, so that IR personnel could examine the findings and be prepared to explain them to others.

While not everyone will agree with this analysis, on balance NSSE's strategy of reminding key institutional leaders about the value of student engagement to the educational process and using data to guide institutional improvement increased the visibility of the IR office. Although this approach occasionally presented challenges, overall it served to strengthen internal communications and working relationships consistent with the goal of enhancing the quality of the undergraduate experience.

## Conclusion

Institutions cannot change who students are when they start college. But with the right assessment tools, colleges can identify areas where improvements in teaching and learning will increase the chances that their students attain their educational and personal goals. NSSE and its two-year counterpart, CCSSE, provide high-quality, behaviorally oriented data about aspects of the student experience that are related to student success. Moreover, the results can be used almost immediately to focus on areas where emphasizing good educational practice could yield more robust student outcomes. In this sense, student engagement is a construct whose time has surely come.

While it is gratifying that engagement is widely recognized as a desirable educational condition, the construct can be misinterpreted and misused. Indeed, proponents of popular ideas sometimes adopt a hegemonic, one-size-fits-all way of thinking. Student engagement is too important, as well as too complicated, for the educational community to allow this to happen. For example, as with other college experiences, engagement tends to have conditional effects, with students with certain characteristics benefiting from some types of activities more so than other students. In addition, the variance within any group of students, such as men and women or African Americans and Latinos, is almost always greater than between the groups (Kuh, 2003, 2008). We must be ever vigilant to be sure we are interpreting and using engagement data appropriately and continue to learn more about what forms of engagement work best under what circumstances for different groups of students. The following chapters in this volume offer guidance toward these and related ends.

## Appendix A: NSSE Consortium and System Participation, 2000–2008

The total years of participation are in parentheses.
Consortia
  American Democracy Project (5)
  Arts Consortium (2)
  Associated New American Colleges (4)
  Association of American Universities Data Exchange (9)
  Association of Independent Colleges of Art and Design (3)
  Association of Independent Technical Universities (4)
  Bringing Theory to Practice (1)
  Canadian Consortium (1)
  Catholic Colleges and Universities (6)
  Colleges That Change Lives (1)
  Committee on Institutional Cooperation (1)
  Concordia Universities (2)
  Council for Christian Colleges and Universities (7)
  Council of Independent Colleges (2)
  Council of Public Liberal Arts Colleges (5)
  Flashlight Group (1)
  G13: Canadian Research Universities (2)
  Hispanic Serving Institutions (1)
  Historically Black Colleges and Universities (2)
  Information Literacy (1)
  Jesuit Colleges and Universities (6)

Lutheran Colleges and Universities (1)
Mid-Atlantic Private Colleges (1)
Military Academy Consortium (1)
Mission Engagement Consortium for Independent Colleges (1)
Online Educators Consortium (1)
Private Liberal Arts Colleges and Universities (6)
Teagle Integrated Learning Consortium (1)
Teagle Writing Grant Consortium (1)
Texas Six (1)
Urban Universities (9)
Women's Colleges (8)
Work Colleges (2)
Systems
California State University (3)
City University of New York (1)
Connecticut State Universities (4)
Indiana University System (1)
Kentucky Council on Postsecondary Education (4)
New Jersey Public Universities (1)
North Dakota University System (2)
Ontario Universities (2)
Pennsylvania State System of Higher Education (1)
Pennsylvania State University (1)
South Dakota Public Universities (5)
State University of New York (1)
Tennessee Publics (1)
Texas A&M System (4)
University of Hawaii (1)
University of Maine (1)
University of Maryland (1)
University of Massachusetts (2)
University of Missouri (5)
University of North Carolina (1)
University of Texas (7)
University of Wisconsin Comprehensives (4)
University System of Georgia (2)

## Appendix B: NSSE Benchmarks

The benchmarks are based on forty-two key questions from the NSSE that capture many of the most important aspects of the student experience. These student behaviors and institutional features are some of the more powerful contributors to learning and personal development.

**Level of Academic Challenge.** Challenging intellectual and creative work is central to student learning and collegiate quality. Colleges and universities promote high levels of student achievement by emphasizing the importance of academic effort and setting high expectations for student performance:

- Preparing for class (studying, reading, writing, rehearsing, and so forth related to academic program)
- Number of assigned textbooks, books, or book-length packs of course readings
- Number of written papers or reports of twenty pages or more; number of written papers or reports of between five and nineteen pages; and number of written papers or reports of fewer than five pages
- Course work emphasizing analysis of the basic elements of an idea, experience, or theory
- Course work emphasizing synthesis and organizing of ideas, information, or experiences into new, more complex interpretations and relationships
- Course work emphasizing the making of judgments about the value of information, arguments, or methods
- Course work emphasizing application of theories or concepts to practical problems or in new situations
- Working harder than you thought you could to meet an instructor's standards or expectations
- Campus environment emphasizing time studying and on academic work

**Active and Collaborative Learning.**  Students learn more when they are intensely involved in their education and asked to think about what they are learning in different settings. Collaborating with others in solving problems or mastering difficult material prepares students for the messy, unscripted problems they will encounter daily during and after college:

- Asked questions in class or contributed to class discussions
- Made a class presentation
- Worked with other students on projects during class
- Worked with classmates outside class to prepare class assignments
- Tutored or taught other students
- Participated in a community-based project as part of a regular course
- Discussed ideas from your readings or classes with others outside class (students, family members, coworkers, or others)

**Student-Faculty Interaction.**  Students learn firsthand how experts think about and solve practical problems by interacting with faculty members inside and outside the classroom. As a result, their teachers become role models, mentors, and guides for continuous, life-long learning:

- Discussed grades or assignments with an instructor
- Talked about career plans with a faculty member or advisor
- Discussed ideas from your readings or classes with faculty members outside class

- Worked with faculty members on activities other than course work (committees, orientation, student-life activities, and so forth)
- Received prompt feedback from faculty on your academic performance (written or oral)
- Worked with a faculty member on a research project outside of class

**Enriching Educational Experiences.** Complementary learning opportunities in and out of class augment academic programs. Diversity experiences teach students valuable things about themselves and others. Technology facilitates collaboration between peers and instructors. Internships, community service, and senior capstone courses provide opportunities to integrate and apply knowledge:

- Participating in cocurricular activities (organizations, publications, student government, sports, and so forth)
- Practicum, internship, field experience, co-op experience, or clinical assignment
- Community service or volunteer work
- Foreign language course work
- Study abroad
- Independent study or self-designed major
- Culminating senior experience (comprehensive exam, capstone course, thesis, project, and so on)
- Serious conversations with students of different religious beliefs, political opinions, or personal values
- Serious conversations with students of a different race or ethnicity
- Using electronic technology to discuss or complete an assignment
- Campus environment encouraging contact among students from different economic, social, and racial or ethnic backgrounds
- Participating in a learning community or some other formal program where groups of students take two or more classes together

**Supportive Campus Environment.** Students perform better and are more satisfied at colleges that are committed to their success and cultivate positive working and social relations among different groups on campus:

- Campus environment provides the support you need to help you succeed academically
- Campus environment helps you cope with your nonacademic responsibilities (work, family, and so on)
- Campus environment provides the support you need to thrive socially
- Quality of relationships with other students
- Quality of relationships with faculty members
- Quality of relationships with administrative personnel and offices

## Notes

1. The members of the design team that Peter Ewell convened to develop the NSSE questionnaire were Alexander Astin, Gary Barnes, Arthur Chickering, John N. Gardner, George Kuh, Richard Light, and Ted Marchese.

2. While engagement in effective educational practices generally benefits all students, the more pronounced effects tend to be conditional and sometimes compensatory (Cruce, Wolniak, Seifert, and Pascarella, 2006; Kuh and others, 2008; Pascarella and Terenzini, 2005). Conditional effects represent differences in the amount of change or development or learning of one group of students relative to other groups. Compensatory effects indicate that students who may start college underprepared in one or more areas benefit differentially compared with their relatively advantaged peers by participating in certain programs or practices. For example, Kuh and others (2008) found that a global measure of engagement (composite score based on eighteen items from NSSE) boosted to a small degree the first-year grade point average of students who entered college with lower levels of academic achievement as well as persistence of African American students.

3. The original NSSE Technical Advisory Panel members were Trudy Banta, Gary Barnes, Emerson Elliot, Peter Ewell (chair), John Gardner, Sylvia Hurtado, John Kennedy, Alex McCormick, Deborah Teeter, and Patrick Terenzini. Gary Pike also began to regularly contribute to efforts to strengthen NSSE psychometrics beginning in 2003.

## References

Astin, A. W. "Student Involvement: A Developmental Theory for Higher Education." *Journal of College Student Development*, 1984, 25(4), 297–308.

Astin, A. W. *What Matters in College? Four Critical Years Revisited.* San Francisco: Jossey-Bass, 1993.

Baird, L. L. *Using Self-Reports to Predict Student Performance.* New York: College Board, 1976.

Chickering, A. W., and Gamson, Z. F. "Seven Principles for Good Practice in Undergraduate Education." *AAHE Bulletin*, Mar. 1987, pp. 3–7.

Commission on the Future of Higher Education. *A Test of Leadership: Charting the Future of U.S. Higher Education.* Washington, D.C.: U.S. Department of Education, 2006. Retrieved Sept. 4, 2008, from http://www.ed.gov/about/bdscomm/list/hiedfuture/reports/final-report.pdf.

Cruce, T., Wolniak, G. C., Seifert, T. A., and Pascarella, E. T. "Impacts of Good Practices on Cognitive Development, Learning Orientations, and Graduate Degree Plans During the First Year of College." *Journal of College Student Development*, 2006, 47(4), 365–383.

Ewell, P. T., and Jones, D. P. *Indicators of "Good Practice" in Undergraduate Education: A Handbook for Development and Implementation.* Boulder, Colo.: National Center for Higher Education Management Systems, 1996.

Kuh, G. D. "Assessing What Really Matters to Student Learning: Inside the National Survey of Student Engagement." *Change*, 2001, 33(3), 10–17, 66.

Kuh, G. D. "What We're Learning About Student Engagement from NSSE." *Change*, 2003, 35(2), 24–32.

Kuh, G. D. *Promises and Pitfalls of Institutional Transparency: First Lessons Learned.* Closing plenary address to the Annual Meeting of Higher Learning Commission, Chicago, Apr. 2008.

Kuh, G. D., Schuh, J. H., Whitt, E. J., and Associates. *Involving Colleges: Successful Approaches to Fostering Student Learning and Personal Development Outside the Classroom.* San Francisco: Jossey-Bass, 1991.

Kuh, G. D., Vesper, N., Connolly, M. R., and Pace, C. R. *College Student Experiences Questionnaire: Revised Norms for the Third Edition.* Bloomington: Indiana University Center for Postsecondary Research and Planning, 1997.

Kuh, G. D., and others. *Student Success in College: Creating Conditions That Matter.* San Francisco: Jossey-Bass, 2005.

Kuh, G. D., and others. "Unmasking the Effects of Student Engagement on College Grades and Persistence." *Journal of Higher Education,* 2008, 79(5), 540–563.

Merwin, J. C. "Historical Review of Changing Concepts of Evaluation." In R. L. Tyler (ed.), *Educational Evaluation: New Roles, New Methods: The Sixty-Eighth Yearbook of the National Society for the Study of Education, Part II.* Chicago: University of Chicago Press, 1969.

National Institute of Education. *Involvement in Learning.* Washington, D.C.: U.S. Department of Education, 1984.

National Survey of Student Engagement. *From Promise to Progress: How Colleges and Universities Are Using Student Engagement Results to Improve Collegiate Quality.* Bloomington: Indiana University Center for Postsecondary Research, 2002.

National Survey of Student Engagement. *A Pocket Guide to Choosing a College: Are You Asking the Right Questions.* Bloomington: Indiana University Center for Postsecondary Research, 2008. Retrieved Jan. 16, 2008, from http://nsse.iub.edu/html/pocket_guide_intro.cfm.

Nelson Laird, T. F., Shoup, R., Kuh, G. D., and Schwarz, M. J. "The Effects of Discipline on Deep Approaches to Student Learning and College Outcomes." *Research in Higher Education,* 2008, 49(6), 469–494.

Pace, C. R. "Measuring the Quality of Student Effort." *Current Issues in Higher Education,* 1980, 2, 10–16.

Pace, C. R. *Measuring the Quality of College Student Experiences: An Account of the Development and Use of the College Student Experiences Questionnaire.* Los Angeles: Higher Education Research Institute, 1984.

Pace, C. R. *The Credibility of Student Self-Reports.* Los Angeles: Center for the Study of Evaluation, University of California, 1985.

Pace, C. R. *The Undergraduates: A Report of Their Activities and College Experiences in the 1980s.* Los Angeles: Center for the Study of Evaluation, UCLA Graduate School of Education, 1990.

Pascarella, E. T. "College Environmental Influences on Learning and Cognitive Development: A Critical Review and Synthesis." In J. C. Smart (ed.), *Higher Education: Handbook of Theory and Research.* New York: Agathon, 1985.

Pascarella, E. T., and Terenzini, P. T. *How College Affects Students: A Third Decade of Research.* San Francisco: Jossey-Bass, 2005.

Pike, G. R. "The Relationship Between Self Reports of College Experiences and Achievement Test Scores." *Research in Higher Education,* 1995, 36(1), 1–21.

Pike, G. R. "The Convergent and Discriminant Validity of NSSE Scalelet Scores." *Journal of College Student Development,* 2006, 47(5), 551–564.

Tinto, V. *Leaving College: Rethinking the Causes and Cures of Student Attrition.* Chicago: University of Chicago Press, 1987.

Tinto, V. *Leaving College: Rethinking the Causes and Cures of Student Attrition.* (2nd ed.) Chicago: University of Chicago Press, 1993.

*GEORGE D. KUH is Chancellor's Professor of Higher Education and director of the Center for Postsecondary Research at Indiana University–Bloomington.*

NEW DIRECTIONS FOR INSTITUTIONAL RESEARCH • DOI: 10.1002/ir

# 2

*A suite of assessment tools, including measures of student engagement, powers a cycle of activities that create an institutional culture of planning and decision making based on evidence.*

# The Use of Engagement Data in Accreditation, Planning, and Assessment

*Trudy W. Banta, Gary R. Pike, Michele J. Hansen*

Indiana University–Purdue University Indianapolis (IUPUI) uses a suite of assessment tools to guide and reinforce a cycle of activities that creates an institutional culture of planning and decision making based on evidence. This cycle includes institutional planning (goal setting), implementation of plans, assessment of outcomes, use of findings to improve processes, and then adjustment of plans to reflect progress or lack thereof (see Figure 2.1). Among the surveys we use is the National Survey of Student Engagement (NSSE).

## Planning/Assessment/Improvement Cycle Encourages Use of Engagement Data

In this chapter, we expand on this cyclical model and illustrate how student engagement data can be used in addressing external requirements for accreditation and accountability and internal needs for strategic planning and program assessment.

**Goal Setting.** The first crucial step in creating a culture based on evidence is to involve stakeholders in a process of identifying goals for student learning and student engagement in the academic programs and support services that are designed to promote learning and development. Of course, individual colleges and departments will have additional goals related to workforce development, scholarship and discovery, community engagement, and other matters, but our focus in this chapter is the student experience in and outside the classroom.

NEW DIRECTIONS FOR INSTITUTIONAL RESEARCH, no. 141, Spring 2009  © Wiley Periodicals, Inc.
Published online in Wiley InterScience (www.interscience.wiley.com) • DOI: 10.1002/ir.284

### Figure 2.1.  Planning, Evaluation, and Improvement at IUPUI

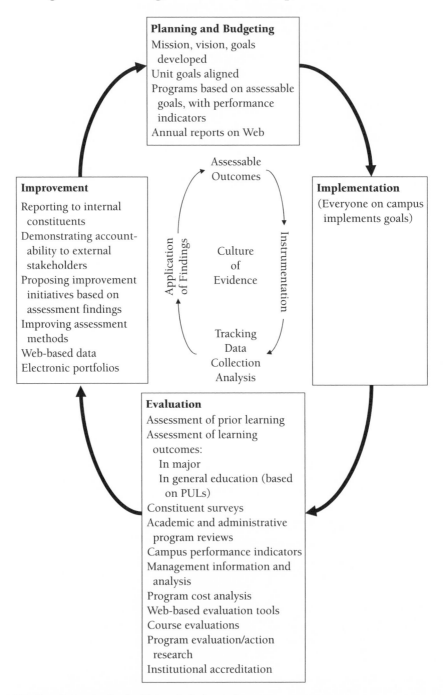

**Planning and Budgeting**
Mission, vision, goals
    developed
Unit goals aligned
Programs based on assessable
    goals, with performance
    indicators
Annual reports on Web

**Improvement**
Reporting to internal
    constituents
Demonstrating account-
    ability to external
    stakeholders
Proposing improvement
    initiatives based on
    assessment findings
Improving assessment
    methods
Web-based data
Electronic portfolios

Assessable
Outcomes

Application
of Findings

Culture
of
Evidence

Instrumentation

Tracking
Data
Collection
Analysis

**Implementation**
(Everyone on campus
    implements goals)

**Evaluation**
Assessment of prior learning
Assessment of learning
    outcomes:
        In major
        In general education (based
        on PULs)
Constituent surveys
Academic and administrative
    program reviews
Campus performance indicators
Management information and
    analysis
Program cost analysis
Web-based evaluation tools
Course evaluations
Program evaluation/action
    research
Institutional accreditation

© Indiana University–Purdue University Indianapolis.

Stakeholders in the planning process include faculty, staff, students, and administrators at all levels. Employers and other community representatives can review the goals being considered, particularly as the planning reaches the level of the academic discipline in which they have a vested interest. Because responsibility for the curriculum belongs to the faculty, goals for student learning in general education and the major must be determined by the faculty. Student affairs professionals are the experts when it comes to cocurricular experiences, making their participation in setting goals for student development vital. Finally, students are the best sources of information about how they perceive and experience the campus environment, and many are eager and willing to share constructive ideas to help shape the curricula to which they are committed and invested.

Institutional research professionals can play a number of important roles in campus planning, from leading the entire initiative to providing data that support particular strategic directions. Yet they should be careful not to underestimate the amount of time it may take to achieve broad consensus on institution-wide goals. At IUPUI, senior campus administrators and deans took no more than six months to agree on the broad goal, "enhance undergraduate student learning and success," and supporting objectives like enhancing honors programming and opportunities for undergraduate research, internships, service-learning, and international experiences (Indiana University–Purdue University Indianapolis, 2002). Then review by faculty, students, and community leaders took another six months or so. But it took faculty eight years to reach agreement on how to implement the goal of constructing "a coherent general education experience for every student"!

**Identifying Assessment Measures.**  Once stakeholders agree on goals and objectives and various offices and departments decide how they will implement the goals, the next step is to connect appropriate evaluative mechanisms to the goals. Ideally, evaluation methods will be considered when developing goals and objectives, but evaluation often takes a back seat during the planning process. The key is to conduct needs assessments and begin tracking progress as soon as possible. Campuses will call on institutional research professionals to do both.

Direct measures such as exams and research papers are supremely important measures of learning experience goals, such as constructing "a coherent general education experience for every student" or providing "experiences that increase student understanding of other cultures." Indirect measures are essential too, however, if we are to understand how students experience the learning opportunities we provide for them and why they are achieving some of our learning objectives and not others. As an indirect measure of these goals, NSSE can contribute valuable data.

**Relating Assessment Findings to Valued Goals.**  If there is widespread involvement in setting institution-wide goals and if senior administrators encourage and recognize their implementation, colleges and universities can establish campuswide committees, and in some cases

New Directions for Institutional Research • DOI: 10.1002/ir

discipline-specific counterparts, to oversee and coordinate programs and activities designed to achieve the goals. Institutional research professionals can serve as staff to campuswide groups charged with implementing important initiatives like general education, advising, and student retention. By attending meetings, listening to deliberations, and contributing ideas for solutions, institutional research staff can determine the kinds of analyses that can yield the information these groups need to inform their decisions.

At IUPUI those eight years of work on an approach to general education yielded six principles that serve as goals for student learning in all majors. These principles of undergraduate learning (PULs) include cross-cutting skills such as oral and written communication and critical thinking, as well as understanding society and cultures, and developing values and ethics. Several campuswide committees oversee the implementation of assessment of student achievement of the PULs, and institutional research professionals serve on these committees in order to understand their data and information needs. IUPUI stakeholders identified NSSE items related to each PUL and are tracking student responses on individual items, as well as scalelets composed of multiple items, over time. Following are some of the items from the NSSE questionnaire used to assess the PULs:

Core Communication and Quantitative Skills
    11c.   Writing clearly and effectively
    11d.   Speaking clearly and effectively
    11f.   Analyzing quantitative problems
    11g.   Using computing and information technology
Critical Thinking
    11e.   Thinking critically and analytically
Integration and Application of Knowledge
    11m. Solving complex real-world problems
Intellectual Depth, Breadth, and Adaptiveness
    11a.   Acquiring a broad general education
    11b.   Acquiring job- or work-related knowledge and skills
    11j.   Learning effectively on your own
Understanding Society and Culture
    11h.   Working effectively with others
Understanding yourself
    11l.   Understanding people of other racial and ethnic backgrounds
Values and Ethics
    11i.   Voting in local, state, or national elections
    11n.   Developing a personal code of values and ethics
    11o.   Contributing to the welfare of your community

**Using Data to Improve Programs and Services.** Ensuring that the campus community actually uses evidence related to the success or failure of goal attainment to make improvements involves implementing all the steps outlined above. Stakeholders must be convinced that institutional goals are sufficiently important to implement. Individuals and committees must be charged with the responsibility to oversee and coordinate implementation activities. Appropriate measures must be connected to each of the goals in order to track progress. Individuals must analyze, interpret, and present data from measurement methods such as administration of the NSSE in ways that shed light on important questions about implementation.

The likelihood that campus community members see assessment data as a guide for improvement action is increased substantially and is an important step for an institution on its way toward developing a culture based on evidence when all of these prerequisites are in place. For example, to further student achievement of the PUL related to effective written communication skills, campus administration appointed the director of campus writing to develop a Writing Across the Curriculum (WAC) program at IUPUI. Stakeholders identified NSSE items to contribute to the evaluation of the effectiveness of the WAC initiative. Evidence that the program improved students' perceptions of their growth as writers, as well as academic self-confidence, which contribute to retention and success, convinced senior academic leaders to continue funding for WAC.

**Communicating Evidence That Assessment Findings Are Used.** It is imperative that institutional research professionals ensure that data are used appropriately to make warranted improvements in instruction, curricula, and student support services. But campuses need to do additional work in order to build a culture based on evidence. It is important to inform students, faculty, and administrators that the institution is using evaluative data to further progress toward institutional goals. These stakeholders must see evidence that the time and resources devoted to evaluation have fulfilled their promise. Institutional research professionals can produce annual progress reports on institutional goals that are disseminated in print and on the Web to community stakeholders, as well as to faculty, staff, and students. They can make periodic brief written and oral reports to faculty and student leaders, academic and student affairs administrators, and campuswide oversight committees. As the campus accumulates evidence that some institution-wide goals have been accomplished or they find that some very lofty goals need to be replaced with interim steps before they can be attained, faculty and administrative leaders will see the value in these processes and will engage in institution-wide planning anew, and the entire planning, assessment, and improvement cycle can begin again.

## Institutional Examples of NSSE Use

Scholarly assessment activities should result in high-quality information that leaders can leverage to demonstrate program effectiveness to external audiences and guide internal policy, program development, and decision making (Kuh, Gonyea, and Rodriguez, 2002). Then campus leaders should

NEW DIRECTIONS FOR INSTITUTIONAL RESEARCH • DOI: 10.1002/ir

communicate assessment information in a way that facilitates ongoing dialogue and active planning among internal and external stakeholders.

NSSE is an especially useful assessment tool for measuring the quality of student experiences and involvement in educationally purposeful activities because of its psychometric properties, provision of normative data, and perceived face value among administrators and faculty. NSSE has been employed by various types of institutions—doctorate-granting universities, master's colleges and universities, and baccalaureate colleges—for numerous purposes, including institutional accreditation, accountability reporting, strategic planning, and program assessment.

**Institutional Accreditation.** NSSE results have become important data elements in many institutions' self-studies for accreditation. In fact, NSSE staff, working with the regional accrediting associations, have mapped questions from the survey to specific accreditation standards for all six regional accrediting associations (see http://nsse.iub.edu/institute/index.cfm?view=tools/accred).

The ways in which institutions have chosen to use NSSE results in the self-study process are varied. For example, Illinois State University used NSSE results to develop goals for its Partnerships for Student Learning emphasis in its self-study for North Central Association reaccreditation. NSSE data continue to play a vital role in the institution's dashboard indicators (see http://www.ilstu.edu/reportcards/dashboard/index.phtml).

In 2003, Mississippi State University (MSU) underwent the decennial Commission on Colleges of the Southern Association of Colleges and Schools (SACS) reaccreditation process, and the visiting team identified several issues to which the university was required to respond. One area of concern was whether MSU faculty members were adequately assessing student outcomes related to the institutional mission. As at many other institutions, the MSU mission statement identifies several student learning outcomes that focus on the public benefits of higher education: citizenship and leadership, tolerance for opposing points of view, a commitment to lifelong learning, and a spirit of inquiry (see http://www.msstate.edu/web/mission.html). Several questions from the NSSE survey elicit information about student learning related to the outcomes, and MSU faculty were able to provide this information to the Commission on Colleges. The university now regularly administers NSSE and uses the resulting data to track student learning and development in these areas.

Skidmore College faculty administered the NSSE survey in 2003 and used the data in their self-study for reaccreditation by the Middle States Commission on Higher Education. After reviewing their NSSE results, Skidmore faculty decided to focus more attention on improving student engagement, particularly for first-year students. The Skidmore strategic plan, Engaged Liberal Learning, focuses on goals for (1) student engagement and academic achievement, (2) intercultural and global understanding, (3) informed, responsible citizenship, and (4) independence and resources (see http://www.skidmore.edu/planning/executive_summary/index.htm).

NEW DIRECTIONS FOR INSTITUTIONAL RESEARCH • DOI: 10.1002/ir

The University of Alabama at Tuscaloosa is also SACS accredited. As part of the core requirements of the Principles of Accreditation, SACS expects colleges and universities to complete a quality enhancement plan (QEP) (Southern Association of Colleges and Schools, 2007). Colleges and universities must develop the plan through an institution-wide process, and it must focus on student learning, have clearly identified goals, and describe a plan for assessing progress toward those goals. University of Alabama faculty selected improving active and collaborative learning on campus as the subject of their QEP based on NSSE results showing that the university had significant opportunities for improvement in these areas. Now the university uses students' responses to the NSSE survey items related to active and collaborative learning to evaluate progress toward its goals. QEP assessments will also make use of item responses on the Faculty Survey of Student Engagement (FSSE) and the Classroom Survey of Student Engagement. In order to increase faculty members' understanding of NSSE, university administrators have scheduled a series of seminars to explain NSSE to faculty members, share the university's NSSE results, and talk about how the results can be used to improve active and collaborative learning on campus (personal communication from Robert Smallwood, Nov. 19, 2007).

The Academic Quality Improvement Plan (AQIP) is one of the approaches to accreditation offered by the Higher Learning Commission of the North Central Association. NSSE data can provide useful information for institutions developing systems portfolios around the nine AQIP categories. NSSE data are perhaps most relevant for AQIP Category 1: Helping Students Learn. Faculty at the University of Indianapolis made extensive use of NSSE data in developing their AQIP systems portfolio. NSSE is also an important element in the University of Indianapolis's current action project focused on facilitating the assessment of university-wide learning goals (see http://aqip.uindy.edu).

**Accountability Reporting.** Colleges and universities can also use NSSE results to satisfy community, state, and federal demands for evidence of accountability. In 2005, University of Wisconsin System administrators issued an accountability report that included assessments of a variety of goals related to access, retention and graduation, student learning, and campus environments. Extensive use of NSSE results helped to gauge the system's progress toward goals related to student learning and the ways in which campus environments help to promote student learning. The final report included NSSE items on advising, critical thinking, interactions with faculty and diverse peers, and study abroad, as well as comparisons to national results. For various reasons, the final report characterized the system as a whole and did not provide results for individual campuses (University of Wisconsin System, 2005).

Members of the South Dakota Board of Regents opted for a different approach when issuing a report on general education based in part on NSSE data. In addition to providing national and systemwide information, the board

NEW DIRECTIONS FOR INSTITUTIONAL RESEARCH • DOI: 10.1002/ir

reported results for all six campuses: Black Hills State University, Dakota State University, Northern State University, South Dakota School of Mines and Technology, South Dakota State University, and the University of South Dakota. The final report also made use of effect size differences to identify institutions that were substantially above or below system averages. The final report included data on selected items from the NSSE sections on academic and intellectual experiences, reading and writing, enriching educational experiences, and educational and personal growth. The board also included data from the 2003 pilot administration of FSSE in the report provided (South Dakota Board of Regents, 2004b). To assist policymakers and other constituents in interpreting the NSSE results, board staff included a guide explaining the relationships between goals for general education programs and questions on NSSE and FSSE (South Dakota Board of Regents, 2004a).

**Strategic Planning.** NSSE can be a robust instrument for assessing progress toward achieving an institution's strategic planning goals. Campus leaders at Oklahoma State University (2002) created a Web site to describe the relationship between NSSE responses and their strategic planning activities (http://uat.okstate.edu/assessment/surveys/student/nsse/2002/concepts/index.htm). They also communicated results to multiple groups across campus (Deans Council, Faculty Council, and Student Affairs Unit Heads) and used results to assess the degree to which the campus met major university goals. OSU leaders urged colleges and departments to administer questions from NSSE to collect additional data at the unit level and on topics related to specific groups of students. OSU Assessment Council members and Office of University Assessment staff made several data-driven recommendations in an effort to fuel the academic planning process. For example, campus leaders encouraged faculty in each undergraduate college to develop a plan to respond to areas of concern identified with NSSE items, particularly those related to Level of Academic Challenge and Enriching Educational Experiences. Academic units were instructed to "use the NSSE results as a guideline" and to "identify strengths and potential areas for improvement regarding student engagement." In addition, leaders encouraged faculty to develop short- and long-term modifications designed to improve student engagement in the areas of academic challenge and enriching educational experiences.

Faculty and staff at Fort Hays State University use NSSE as one of three surveys in their comprehensive planning and assessment efforts. They study NSSE data, along with data from the locally developed General Education/Senior Survey and the Noel-Levitz Student Satisfaction Inventory, to gauge student attainment of learning outcomes, levels of student engagement, and satisfaction with educational programs and services. In 2005, members of the University Assessment Steering Committee reported that NSSE responses had helped them discover an important opportunity for improving students' critical thinking skills. In addition to identifying this need, the NSSE data, in conjunction with other sources of information, helped members of the steering committee develop specific improvement actions. Key

New Directions for Institutional Research • DOI: 10.1002/ir

objectives of the improvement plan were providing professional development opportunities for faculty members to give them better alternatives for
teaching critical thinking skills; increasing students' opportunities to engage
in reflection, application, and analysis in class assignments; and informing
students of the key components of critical thinking.

University of Central Oklahoma faculty and staff incorporate NSSE findings in their ongoing assessment and improvement initiatives. They make use
of several formal quality improvement techniques and processes to assess
NSSE results and identify actions for improvement. A broad-based team
including administrators, deans, and faculty members initially used a Pareto
approach (arranging response frequencies in descending order) to analyze
NSSE results and identify important areas of concern. In subsequent meetings
the action team worked through cause-and-effect (fishbone) diagrams to identify the root causes of problems. In the final report, the action team noted that
"many courses at UCO are not considered rigorous" by students (National
Survey of Student Engagement Action Team, n.d., p. 4). The action team recommended that faculty members require rigorous course work consistent with
state policies and that these expectations be clearly stated on each course syl-
labus. Team members also recommended that the university enhance student
support systems in order to create a culture of support for student success.

Often when campus stakeholders convene to identify goals for student
learning and student engagement and plan academic programs and support
services to enhance student development, there is an explicit or implicit focus
on increasing student persistence. As higher education continues to experience declining levels of resources, campuses will continue to give attention to
increasing the rates at which students persist and graduate (Tinto, 2006–2007).
NSSE results appear to have substantial utility in creating deeper levels of
understanding about the intervening variables that contribute to persistence
and retention. Humboldt State University administered NSSE to freshmen to
help determine why students were withdrawing from the institution (Hughes
and Pace, 2003). Students who withdrew had lower levels of engagement in
several areas, including classroom learning, faculty interactions, and cocurricular activities. The university used these findings to guide conversations
between advisors and students, as well as to alert faculty and staff about critical areas they needed to address in order to improve retention rates.

Assessment scholars recommend employing multiple methods and
obtaining evidence from multiple sources to obtain a comprehensive understanding of student progress, success, and institutional performance. In an
effort to explore how minority-serving institutions prepare significant numbers of students of color and provide quality academic experiences, several
groups joined together to integrate NSSE data with other sources of information to assess levels of student engagement and institutional performance
(Bridges, Cambridge, Kuh, and Leegwater, 2005). The Building Engagement
and Attainment of Minority Students project, a multiyear joint initiative of
the American Association for Higher Education and the NSSE, funded by

Lumina Foundation for Education, is a national partnership designed to reduce the gap in higher education attainment for African Americans, Hispanics, and American Indians by increasing the numbers of these students who achieve their educational objectives. Project representatives convened a roundtable discussion and decided to administer NSSE and provide analytical support to minority-serving institutions. According to Bridges, Cambridge, Kuh, and Leegwater, "each participating institution will administer the NSSE survey twice, develop action plans for improving areas revealed through survey results, track and report on improvement, and work with similar campuses in benchmarking groups to share best practices, offer feedback on institutional action plans, and establish student engagement and learning trends across multiple campuses" (2005, p. 32). The authors also cite Norfolk State University as an example of an institution where NSSE scores revealed a need to focus on incoming students. Subsequently faculty and staff devoted a year attempting to understand Norfolk State students and the campus environment. Norfolk State leaders determined that freshman support initiatives needed to be planned and coordinated more effectively. They instituted a more intentional, holistic approach to academic life for their first-year students.

**Program Assessment.** NSSE results can also be useful in assessing the value of educational programs. In a comprehensive study, researchers used NSSE results to demonstrate how learning communities enhance social and intellectual development and help build a sense of community among college students (Zhao and Kuh, 2004). The investigators assessed student engagement levels of first-year and senior students from 365 four-year institutions, controlling for student and institutional characteristics. Results suggested that participating in learning communities was positively associated with academic performance, engagement in educationally productive activities (academic integration, active and collaborative learning, and interaction with faculty members), and overall satisfaction with the college experience. This study yielded sought-after evidence that learning communities have value-added effects for participating students. It has compelled academic leaders at many colleges and universities to assess how many and what types of learning communities are operating on their campuses and the numbers of students participating in them. In addition, the study provided support for the implementation of learning communities to meet the diverse needs of students.

At IUPUI, NSSE has served as a critical source of evidence for planning, monitoring, assessing, and improving themed learning communities (TLCs). In 2003, University College faculty members and administrators formed TLCs by linking at least three first-year courses in a structured first-semester learning environment where students could develop a strong sense of community and integrate their learning across disciplines. In themed learning communities, instructors collaborate in advance to select a theme and develop common learning experiences. The broad goal of advancing student learning and success guided the development of TLCs. Soon after implementing TLCs, faculty, administrators, advisors, and staff began an iterative and collaborative planning process of articulating more specific goals and curriculum objectives. Planning committee members articulated institutional goals such as improving retention and graduation rates, as well as strategies focused on student-level outcomes like the following: form learning support networks, enhance contact with a network of faculty and staff, improve active and collaborative learning, understand the value of diversity by exposure to multiple points of view, apply classroom learning to the real world, understand the relationship between academic learning and cocurricular activities, and integrate learning across academic and professional disciplines.

Once faculty members agreed on the goals and learning objectives, they decided how to structure learning environments to accomplish the goals. They consulted with institutional researchers and assessment directors to determine what sources of evidence could serve as appropriate measures of goal attainment. In addition to advocating the use of quantitative outcome measures such as grade point averages, one-year persistence rates, graduation rates, and direct measures of student learning such as common writing assignments and graded assignments, institutional researchers and assessment directors promoted other indirect measures of student learning, such as the locally developed Continuing Student Satisfaction and Priorities Survey and NSSE, as effective mechanisms for tracking the effectiveness of TLCs. NSSE was an obvious choice because several items were closely aligned with the agreed-on goals and the instrument provided faculty members with normative data. TLC faculty members and administrators were particularly interested in the availability of comparative data.

During several years of implementing TLCs and developing the program, NSSE results helped to foster understanding of how students were experiencing the TLCs and, most important, provided some sense about why TLC students were achieving higher grade point averages and one-year retention rates compared to nonparticipating students, even while controlling for student academic preparation and background characteristics. Members of the campus community conducted a series of analyses to determine if there were significant differences between first-year students participating in TLCs and nonparticipating first-year students on specific items related to TLC goals. Faculty members preferred item-level analyses over NSSE benchmark analyses because of the level of specificity provided by the individual items.

Results suggested that TLC students were significantly more likely than nonparticipants to work on a paper or project that required integrating ideas or information from various sources; to be in courses that include diverse perspectives (different races, religions, genders, and political beliefs, for example) in class discussions or writing assignments; to put together ideas or concepts from different courses when completing assignments or during class discussions; to work harder than they thought they could to meet an instructor's standards or expectations; to try to understand someone else's views by imagining how an issue looks from his or her perspective; and to learn something that changed the way they understood an issue or concept. NSSE responses also indicated that TLC students were more likely to report more institutional emphasis on (1) providing the support needed to help students succeed academically; (2) encouraging contact among students from different economic, social, and racial or ethnic backgrounds; (3) helping students cope with nonacademic responsibilities such as work and family; (4) working effectively with others; and (5) understanding people of other racial/ethnic backgrounds. IUPUI first-year students participating in TLCs also reported higher levels than selected peers on several items that demonstrate the value of TLCs in helping students develop a strong sense of community and see connections across disciplines.

Positive NSSE results and other studies demonstrating that TLC students report greater engagement with college, have higher GPAs, and are retained to the second year at higher rates than non-TLC students led to the expansion of the TLC program from seven TLCs in fall 2003 to twenty-six in fall 2007. These outcomes also have encouraged faculty participation from a growing array of disciplines. New TLCs offered in fall 2007 include African-American Perspectives, Crime in America, and Health and Wellness, as well as TLCs for prospective engineering and business majors. Thus, NSSE results are an important source of evidence for proving as well as improving TLCs. The campus continues to distribute results to faculty team members to guide future planning. Faculty members have leveraged findings to make improvements such as creating more common writing assignments to enhance theme integration across disciplines, implementing more cocurricular activities to improve students' levels of interaction with faculty members and other students, and expanding the TLC program to reach more students.

Most institutions are awash in data, and it is up to busy administrators, institutional researchers, faculty members, and staff to use them effectively to guide improvement efforts. Drawing on interviews with two dozen faculty and staff from various institutions who were responsible for administering NSSE on their respective campuses, Ahren, Ryan, and Massa-McKinley (2008) provide principles to guide practice in five areas: (1) collaborating on the analysis and communication of results, (2) triangulating data, (3) using data to learn more about students, (4) using data to demonstrate goal achievement, and (5) enhancing the first-year experience. According to these authors, more meaningful data-based decision making and action took place when these principles were applied. For example, when campuses employed the principle of collaboration and many stakeholders were actively involved in using NSSE results to determine if academic programs and services met

New Directions for Institutional Research • DOI: 10.1002/ir

intended goals, they were more likely to change and improve local programming. NSSE also can be an important source of information when attempting to confirm that there is a consistent message across many institutional research studies; this triangulation can provide impetus for using data in making critical decisions. Finally, NSSE data can provide guidance for improving first-year programs by deepening understanding of the influence of these programs on students' engagement and satisfaction levels. The campus leaders cited in the examples throughout this chapter appear to have embraced these principles as they are using NSSE data as one source of evidence to develop data-driven plans to improve educational experiences for students at all levels. They are fully engaged in the planning, assessment, and improvement cycle (see Figure 2.1) that we described at the start of this chapter.

## References

Ahren, C., Ryan, H. G., and Massa-McKinley, R. "Assessment Matters: The Why and How of Cracking Open and Using Assessment Results." *About Campus*, 2008, *13*(2), 29–32.

Bridges, B. K., Cambridge, B., Kuh, G. D., and Leegwater, L. H. "Student Engagement at Minority-Serving Institutions: Emerging Lessons from the BEAMS Project." In G. H. Gaither (ed.), *Minority Retention: What Works*. New Directions for Institutional Research, no. 25, San Francisco: Jossey-Bass, 2005.

Hughes, R., and Pace, R. C. "Using NSSE to Study Student Retention and Withdrawal." *Assessment Update*, 2003, *15*(4).

Indiana University–Purdue University Indianapolis. "IUPUI Mission, Vision, Values, Goals, and Objectives." 2002. Retrieved Dec. 3, 2007, from http://www.planning.iupui.edu/planning/.

Kuh, G. D., Gonyea, R. M., and Rodriguez, D. P. "The Scholarly Assessment of Student Development." In T. W. Banta and Associates (eds.), *Building a Scholarship of Assessment*. San Francisco: Jossey-Bass, 2002.

National Survey of Student Engagement Action Team. *Opportunities for Improvement Report*. Edmond, Okla.: Office of Assessment, University of Central Oklahoma, n.d.

Oklahoma State University. "NSSE: A Tool for Strategic Planning and Assessment." 2002. Retrieved Nov. 16, 2007, from http://uat.okstate.edu/assessment/surveys/student/nsse/2002/concepts/index.htm.

South Dakota Board of Regents. "General Education and NSSE." 2004a. Retrieved Jan. 26, 2009 from http://www.sdbor.edu/administration/academics/gen_ed/Gen_Ed_NSSE_2-17-04-Revised.doc.

South Dakota Board of Regents. "General Education and NSSE." 2004b. Retrieved Jan. 26, 2009 from http://www.sdbor.edu/administration/academics/gen_ed/Gen_Ed_NSSE_Selected_info_2-17-04.xls.

Southern Association of Colleges and Schools. "Principles of Accreditation: Foundations of Quality Enhancement (Interim Edition)." 2007. Retrieved Nov. 23, 2007, from http://www.sacscoc.org/pdf/2007%20Interim%20Principles%20complete.pdf.

Tinto, V. "Research and Practice of Student Retention: What Next?" *Journal of College Student Retention*, 2006–2007, *8*(1), 1–19.

University Assessment Steering Committee, Fort Hays State University. "2005 Comprehensive Assessment Report and Strategic Plan." 2005. Retrieved Nov. 23, 2007, from http://www.fhsu.edu/aqip/reports_documents/ascplan.pdf.

University of Wisconsin System "Achieving Excellence: Accountability Report 2004–2005." 2005. Retrieved Nov. 23, 2007, from http://www.uwsa.edu/opar/accountability/achieve05/ae05.pdf.

Zhao, C., and Kuh, G. D. "Adding Value: Learning Communities and Student Engagement." *Research in Higher Education*, 2004, *45*(2), 115–138.

*TRUDY W. BANTA is professor of higher education and senior advisor to the chancellor for academic planning and evaluation at Indiana University–Purdue University Indianapolis.*

*GARY R. PIKE is executive director of information management and institutional research at Indiana University–Purdue University Indianapolis.*

*MICHELE J. HANSEN is director of assessment for University College at Indiana University–Purdue University Indianapolis.*

NEW DIRECTIONS FOR INSTITUTIONAL RESEARCH • DOI: 10.1002/ir

3

*Drawing on their experience, current and former NSSE research analysts offer helpful tips and recommendations for institutional researchers on how to analyze student engagement data, including ways to work with multiple years of results and interpret effect sizes.*

# Analyzing and Interpreting NSSE Data

*Pu-Shih Daniel Chen, Robert M. Gonyea,
Shimon A. Sarraf, Allison BrckaLorenz,
Ali Korkmaz, Amber D. Lambert,
Rick Shoup, Julie M. Williams*

Colleges and universities in the United States are being challenged to assess student outcomes and the quality of programs and services (McPherson and Shulenburger, 2006; Commission on the Future of Higher Education, 2006). One of the more widely used sources of evidence is student engagement as measured by a cluster of student engagement surveys administered by the Center for Postsecondary Research at Indiana University. They include the National Survey of Student Engagement (NSSE) and its companion projects: the Beginning College Survey of Student Engagement, Faculty Survey of Student Engagement, and Law School Survey of Student Engagement. The University of Texas–Austin hosts the two-year variation of the NSSE, the Community College Survey of Student Engagement.

With more than thirteen hundred colleges and universities using NSSE, many institutional researchers may benefit from guidance about how to understand and use these data. This chapter shares practical tips and recommendations for the analysis and interpretation of NSSE data. We divided the chapter into three parts. The first offers six overarching tips and recommendations for working with student engagement data. We then discuss considerations for the analysis of multiple years of student engagement data. Finally, we describe how effect sizes can be used and interpreted to make student engagement results more meaningful.

New Directions for Institutional Research, no. 141, Spring 2009 © Wiley Periodicals, Inc.
Published online in Wiley InterScience (www.interscience.wiley.com) • DOI: 10.1002/ir.285

Although we use NSSE data and examples throughout the chapter, institutional researchers can almost always extrapolate the suggestions we provide to other student experience surveys. Instead of technical discussions of such topics as scale construction and factor analysis, we focus on practical, concrete data manipulations and applications for the analytical work of the institutional research professional.

## Helpful Tips for Analyzing Student Engagement Data

The primary objective of collecting student engagement data is to discover areas where colleges and universities can improve the quality of the student experience. Student experiences and outcomes vary more among students within an institution than the average student varies between institutions (Kuh, 2003; National Survey of Student Engagement, 2008; Pascarella and Terenzini, 2005). While between-institution analyses emphasize average student performance, within-institution data almost always yield more actionable results. This can be achieved by drilling down into results from subgroups such as men and women or students who participate in certain programs or major in different fields of study.

To help inform improvement efforts, institutional researchers must make engagement results accessible and the reports easy to digest. Toward these ends, this section offers six general recommendations to guide the analysis and reporting of student engagement data to campus leaders and other stakeholders.

**Determine the Quality of Institutional Data.** When using engagement results to assess the campus experience or inform a particular campus policy, it is necessary to verify that population estimates derived from the data are accurate and precise. In general, data quality is tied to sample size: the more respondents, the more confident one can be in results. Yet short of a 100 percent response rate, no single indicator provides sufficient evidence that a population estimate is truly unbiased. Below we describe the primary data quality measures an institutional researcher should consider in evaluating data quality.

*Response Rate. Response rate* is the percentage of a sample that completes the questionnaire. Although conventional wisdom holds that the higher the response rate, the better, we encourage a more nuanced exploration of the issue. This conventional view rests on assumptions about nonrespondents. Are they different from respondents and, if so, by how much? *Nonresponse bias,* one potential source of inaccurate population estimates, is a function of both response rate and *nonresponse effect,* the extent to which responders and nonresponders differ on the survey variables of interest (Federal Committee on Statistical Methodology, 2001). Although low response rates may suggest a potential bias in survey estimates of overall population values, they do not necessarily represent bias. As Groves (2006) claims, "There is little empirical support for the notion that low response rate surveys de facto produce estimates with high nonresponse bias" (p. 670). However, when low response rates are coupled with a nonresponse effect, legitimate concerns about bias are warranted. In fact, even high response rates can result in substantial nonresponse bias when linked with large nonresponse effects. Korkmaz and Gonyea (2008) found only trivial differences between precollege characteristics and academic behaviors among NSSE responders and nonresponders, suggesting that nonresponse bias may be trivial. Studies of nonresponse bias by NSSE in 2001 and 2005 also concluded that nonresponse effects are minimal (National Survey of Student Engagement, 2008). Still, as with all other survey results, institutions may vary greatly in terms of nonresponse effects and bias. So under certain conditions, very low response rates may render the results problematic, especially after careful consideration of other data quality measures.

*Sampling Error.* According to Salant and Dillman (1994) sampling error is a fact of life for those using survey data. Sampling error occurs when respondents represent a subset, or sample, of the total population. It estimates how much respondents could differ on survey measures from the entire population of students at an institution. For example, if 60 percent reply "very often" to a particular item and the sampling error is estimated at plus or minus 5 percent, then the actual population value is likely to be between 55 and 65 percent. Estimating sampling error is a function of the number of students who responded to the survey ($n$) and the total number of students in your population ($N$) (see equation 3.1):

$$e = \sqrt{\frac{.9604(N-n)}{n(N-1)}} \tag{3.1}$$

Increasing the number of respondents relative to the total population reduces sampling error. Smaller sampling errors such as ±3 or 5 percent are preferred, although data with larger sampling errors (such as ±10 percent) need not be dismissed offhand but rather interpreted more conservatively.

Sampling error is based on the population of interest. Therefore, to estimate the sampling error for first-year male students, one must base the analysis on the number of all first-year male students in the population and the number of first-year male respondents.

*Proportional Representation.* It is also necessary to determine the extent to which respondent demographics match those of the population. If students with certain characteristics make up 70 percent of the campus population but only 40 percent of the survey respondents, researchers may need to make adjustments, especially if that variable is related to engagement. Weighting or other statistical procedures may counter the potential biases in the data. For instance, NSSE weights its data by gender and enrollment status, not only because women and full-time students respond at higher rates, but also because they respond differently to important NSSE measures. Weighting also helps determine whether changes from year to year

NEW DIRECTIONS FOR INSTITUTIONAL RESEARCH • DOI: 10.1002/ir

can be linked to such things as changing student demographics or campus initiatives.

**Collapse Response Categories for Reporting and Analysis.** Institutional reports of student experiences typically are too detailed to pass along to campus leaders. A task of the institutional researcher is to extract from the raw data and basic reports the most meaningful and relevant pieces of information. One particularly useful approach is to collapse the response categories for individual items into fewer categories in order to succinctly convey results (Table 3.1). For example, the response set "never, sometimes, often, very often" can be recoded so that "very often" and "often" are combined into a new category labeled "frequently." Other times you may simply want to examine the percentage of students who report that they "never" do something.

This approach works when using descriptive analyses to identify percentage differences between subgroups. This technique also is instructive when doing more sophisticated statistical analyses, such as logistic regression to predict students who will participate in high-impact activities (Kuh, 2008).

By collapsing response options using the suggestions in Table 3.1 or other similar methods, institutional researchers can more easily review the results and look for interesting findings to present to decision makers.

**Combine Questions into Workable Scales.** As with any other set of behavioral or attitudinal constructs, student engagement cannot be measured with a ruler or thermometer as we would with some physical characteristics. As a result, questionnaires often include series of questions to gauge student behaviors and attitudes. Yet the responses to a single question may be too narrow for decision making on broader policies, while results from dozens of individual questions may be mixed and inconclusive. Thus, it is useful to combine individual items into scales that consist of a limited number of conceptually related questions. Scales reduce the number of variables in analytical models, may have better reliability, and ultimately may convey more meaningful information than individual questions.

In addition to the five benchmarks of effective educational practice (see Chapter One, this volume, for a description of the benchmarks), NSSE analysts confirmed a deep learning scale of twelve questions with three subscales (Nelson Laird, Shoup, and Kuh, 2006; Nelson Laird, Garver, Niskodé-Dossett, and Banks, 2008). The NSSE instrument also contains three self-reported gains scales based on sixteen questions about the extent that the student's experience at the institution contributed to his or her learning and growth. In addition, Pike (2006a, 2006b) identified eleven useful "scalelets." (SPSS syntax for creating these NSSE scales can be found at www.nsse.iub.edu/html/syntax_library.cfm.)

*Computing Scale Scores.* The simplest method to compute the scale score is to sum the response values for each of the individual items. For example,

### Table 3.1.  Collapsing Response Options with NSSE Data

| New Category | Original Response(s) Used | Sample Question | Recommended Uses |
|---|---|---|---|
| Frequently | "Very often" and "often" | How often have you asked questions in class or contributed to class discussions? | Pinpoint activities students do most on campus; look at percentage differences among subgroups. |
| Never | "Never" | How often have you made a class presentation? | Identify possible areas in need of improvement. |
| Substantial | "Very much" and "quite a bit" | How much has your course work emphasized memorizing facts or ideas? | Examine the amount that course work emphasizes higher-order learning activities, gauge aspects of the campus environment, and look at self-reported gains. |
| Done | "Done" | Have you done or do you plan to study abroad before you graduate? | Report how many students participate in high-impact practices; break down by academic major. |
| Friendly or helpful | Combine top three positive responses on a scale of 1 to 7 | What is the quality of your relationships with other students [or with faculty members]? | Summarize students' relationships with key campus groups—students, faculty, and administrators. |
| Sixteen or more hours | Combine all responses greater than "11–15" hours | How many hours do you spend in a typical seven-day week preparing for class? | Collapse responses for each item differently to create the most useful responses. |
| Quartiles, or above- and below-average groups | All benchmark values recoded into four equal groups, or two groups divided by the mean | Benchmarks, scales, or other continuous measures | Investigate if certain subgroups are over- or underrepresented. For example, if 20 percent of the top quartile is male but males are 40 percent of the entire sample, you can claim male underrepresentation in this high-performing quartile. |

when combining five items that are coded 1 = never, 2 = sometimes, 3 = often, and 4 = very often, the sum will have a minimum score of 5 and a maximum score of 20. A better option may be to compute the mean score for these items, so that the scale score remains within the original range (1 to 4) and can be interpreted according to original response units. For example, a mean score of 3.1 is about an average response of "often."

In some situations, a researcher may need to combine items from different response sets and value ranges. For example, two items might have a range of 1 to 4, and three items might have a range of 1 to 7. If one simply sums or averages the response values to score the scale, the questions with the greater number of options will have a larger influence on the overall score. To balance the contribution of the individual questions, standardize them with a mean of 0 and a standard deviation of 1, and then sum the standard scores. Another option is to recode the individual response values into a common scale range like the NSSE research team does in creating the benchmark, deep learning, gains, and other scale scores. To do so, NSSE converts each item into a scale of 0 to 100, an arbitrarily chosen range for reporting purposes, using equation 3.2:

$$[(\text{response value} - 1)/(\text{total number of response values} - 1)] * 100 \quad (3.2)$$

For example, an item with four response options is converted to 0, 33.3, 66.7, and 100. Afterward, compute the scale score by computing the mean of the mean of these recoded items.

When two scales share a common item (or set of items), be sure not to enter them into the same statistical models or equations. The common item or items will produce artificially higher correlations and confound the statistical analysis.

**Compute Basic Statistical Comparisons Against Published Norms.** In this section, we discuss how institutional researchers can analyze their data for statistical differences against published aggregates and what these findings mean in a practical sense. Although more advanced methods are available, the approaches presented here are offered as shorthand calculations to produce results with a few simple computations.

*Statistical Difference: Calculating* t-*Tests.* The *t*-test determines whether the means of two groups are statistically different from one another, that is, the likelihood that the difference between groups occurred by chance alone. To calculate a *t*-test, one just needs a few descriptive statistics. Equation 3.3 can be used to calculate a *t* score, where $M_1$ is the mean score for the selected institution, $M_2$ is the mean score for the comparison group, and *SEM* is the standard error of the mean:

$$t = \frac{M_1 - M_2}{SEM} \quad (3.3)$$

This definition of SEM is used in one-sample $t$-tests that consider the comparison group to be a population parameter, not a sample estimate. With the exception of extremely small sample sizes, $t$ values greater than 2.0 can be interpreted to mean that a statistically significant difference exists at the $p < .05$ level. Similarly, $t$ values greater than 2.6 imply significance at the $p < .01$ level, and $t$ values greater than 3.3 imply significance at the $p < .001$ level:

For example, an institution may be concerned about the quality of relationships between students and faculty, a NSSE item that is coded on a seven-point rating scale from 1 = "unfriendly, unsupportive, sense of alienation" to 7 = "friendly, supportive, sense of belonging." At the institution, 466 seniors answered this question with a mean of 5.7 and SEM of .06. The mean for all seniors who completed this item in 2008 was 5.4, which can be obtained from the NSSE's Web site. The statistical significance can be determined by calculating the $t$ value as follows.

$$t = \frac{M_1 - M_2}{SEM} = \frac{5.7 - 5.4}{.06} = 5.31$$

Because the $t$ value is greater than 3.3, it indicates that the institutional mean is significantly greater than the NSSE average at the $p < .001$ level.

*Practical Difference: Calculating Effect Size.* An effect size, considered a measure of practical significance, is any measure of the strength of the relationship between two variables. For the purposes of this chapter, we use Cohen's $d$ (Cohen, 1988), the difference between two means divided by the standard deviation of a comparison (or norm) group (or, alternatively, the pooled standard deviation of the two groups). The $d$ statistic expresses the mean difference in standard units and can be interpreted in relative terms. Later in this chapter, we discuss the interpretation of effect sizes in more detail.

Computing an effect size can be particularly helpful for institutions and comparison groups with large sample sizes. Significance tests can be problematic with studies that include large sample sizes because as sample size increases, standard errors of the mean decrease, and thus significance tests more easily yield higher $t$ values. The effect size does not have this limitation, so all comparisons, even those with large sample sizes, can be interpreted in the same general way from a practical standpoint. To calculate effect sizes between an institution's results and a published norm, use equation 3.4, where $M_1$ is the institutional mean, $M_2$ is the norm group mean, and $SD$ is the standard deviation of the norm group:

$$d = \frac{M_1 - M_2}{SD} \tag{3.4}$$

Using the same example as above, the institution's mean for the quality of student relationships variable for seniors was 5.7, the NSSE average for all senior participants in 2008 was 5.4, and the standard deviation for all senior participants in 2008 was 1.4. Applying equation 3.3, the effect size is:

$$d = \frac{M_1 - M_2}{SD} = \frac{5.7 - 5.4}{1.4} = .22$$

Thus, while the t-test revealed that the quality of student relationships with faculty members at the institution was significantly higher than the NSSE average, the effect size shows that the difference is substantive but perhaps small.

**Test for Interaction Effects.** When looking at student differences within survey results, the number of subgroups can be daunting, and drilling down can create too many results to be practically considered in policy development. In addition, dividing the data by a large number of sub-groups has the potential to diminish the statistical power of the analysis. To avoid some of these pitfalls, researchers can test for the existence of inter-action effects, variously termed *conditional, joint, contingency,* or *moderating effects.* Pascarella and Terenzini (2005) emphasized the importance of study-ing conditional effects and urged scholars to take such effects into account in future research. As illustrated in Figure 3.1, an interaction is present when the association between two variables ($X_1$ and $Y$) depends on changes in a third variable ($X_2$) (Agresti and Finlay, 1999).

For example, to see if an interaction exists in the effects of gender and majoring in a science, technology, engineering, and mathematics (STEM) field on student-faculty interaction, one may chart the means of each sub-group (male/female, and STEM/non-STEM). It appears in Figure 3.2 that the effect of gender on student-faculty interaction is different for STEM and non-STEM majors at this institution. Non-STEM females are more likely than their male counterparts to interact with faculty, while the inverse is true in the STEM fields.

*Test for Significant Interactions.* When the two independent variables are categorical as shown in Figure 3.2, the analysis of variance (ANOVA) procedure includes a test of interaction effects among the independent vari-ables. When one or both of the independent variables are continuous, enter-

**Figure 3.1.  Interaction Effect Model**

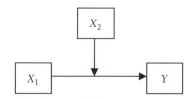

**Figure 3.2. Student-Faculty Interaction by Gender
and Discipline at One Institution**

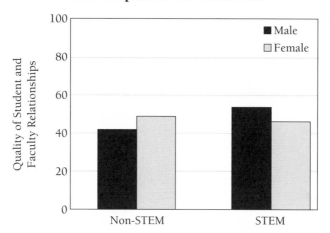

ing cross-product terms into a regression model can test for interactions. For example, if the hypothesis is that the effect of frequent conversations with diverse individuals $(X_1)$ on the quality of student relationships $(Y)$ depends on the student's race $(X_2)$, one can test the hypothesis by creating a cross-product term (for example, $X_1 * X_2$) that represents the possible interactions between race (dummy coded) and conversations with diverse others. This is done by multiplying each of the dummy race variables by the "conversations" variable.

To illustrate, we will look at just two race categories, African American and white, where the African American variable $(X_2)$ is entered into the model and white is left out as the reference group. The interaction term $(X_1 * X_2)$ is entered separately at the end of the regression model so the researcher can look for a significant change in the amount of variance explained (change in $R^2$). If the change is significant, the interaction term explains at least some additional variance, and the main-effects-only model may not be sufficient. In the model without the interaction term, the coefficients represent the effects on the dependent variable while taking all other independent variables into account. With an interaction term in the model, the interpretation changes so that the coefficient is the effect on the dependent variable when the other independent variable is equal to one (Jaccard and Turrisi, 2003). In other words, the coefficients for the variables represent conditional relationships, not main effects. These conditional effects can be calculated by substituting zeros for the dummy variables and creating separate regression equations for each subgroup. This process has the same effect as fitting separate regression lines for each group.

NEW DIRECTIONS FOR INSTITUTIONAL RESEARCH • DOI: 10.1002/ir

**Table 3.2.  Regression Coefficients for
Conversations with Diverse Others,
Being African American, and Interaction
Term on Quality of Student Relationships**

|  | Parameter | Estimate |
|---|---|---|
| $\alpha$ | Intercept | −.02 |
| $x_1$ | Conversations with diverse others | .20 |
| $x_2$ | African American | −.06 |
| $(x_1 * x_2)$ | Conversations * African American | .09 |

Using data from one NSSE institution, Table 3.2 presents illustrative model coefficients, including the interaction term effect. Because these coefficients are conditional and not main effects, separate equations for each race are computed (Table 3.3) (white is indicated when the African American variable is set to zero). The nonparallel slopes in Figure 3.3 indicate that more frequent conversations with diverse others have a stronger effect on the quality of student relationships for African American students than it does for white students.

Examining interaction effects provides administrators and faculty members more specific information as to those students who are more or less engaged and the degree to which they develop desired skills and competencies.

**Link Engagement Data to Other School Records.**  All surveys are limited in the amount of information they provide, so it can be fruitful to link survey data with other student records for a more comprehensive understanding of student engagement and learning on campus. To make this possible, NSSE returns data to institutions with unique student identifiers that institutions provided beforehand in their student population files.

For example, institutional researchers can link high school grades and standardized test scores typically collected during the admission process with students' NSSE responses to determine whether first-year students from different educational backgrounds engage in educationally purposeful activities in comparable ways. While students who achieved lower grades

**Table 3.3.  Summary of Prediction Equation Allowing
Interaction for the Effects of Serious Conversations
on Quality of Student Relationships**

| Race | Y Intercept | Slope | Regression Equation |
|---|---|---|---|
| White | −.02 | .20 | $Y = -.02 + .20x$ |
| African American | −.02 − .06 | .20 + .09 | $Y = -.08 + .29x$ |

**Figure 3.3.  Race Variations in the Effect of Serious Conversations on Supportive Campus Environment**

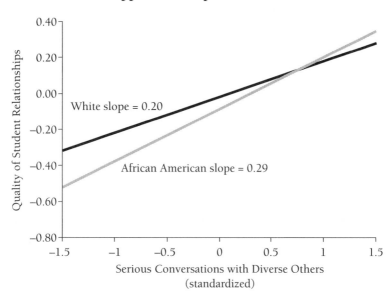

in high school may be less well prepared for college-level work, it may concern faculty and staff to learn that such students also spend fewer hours studying, read less, and are less likely to write multiple drafts of a paper, all of which also could lead to poor performance in college. If such a gap is known, institutions can take action to promote a better understanding of the amount and type of work that is expected for success in the first year. They may offer additional academic enrichment sessions during orientation for students more likely to struggle academically, emphasize good practice in writing and reading in entry-level first-year classes, and reach out to students with lower high school achievement through academic support service centers.

Institutional researchers can also link data about persistence, financial aid, and student satisfaction with survey results to evaluate the effectiveness of specific academic departments or divisions, special academic programs, and student affairs activities. For example, one could examine the first-year engagement patterns of NSSE respondents who reenroll as sophomores to determine which characteristics or activities were associated with persistence. If working more than twenty-five hours per week off campus has a negative relationship with persistence, administrators might reexamine the number of work-study positions available on campus, review how scholarship dollars are distributed, and caution students through orientation and advising activities against working too many hours while enrolled.

**Table 3.4. Examples of Student Records to Link
with Engagement Data**

| Source | Description | Sample Questions for Analysis |
|---|---|---|
| Admissions | High school grades, standardized test scores, high school attended | Do students of varying academic backgrounds report similar levels of academic effort? |
| Financial aid | Scholarship award designations, student need | Are elite academic scholarship winners engaged in more deep learning and research with faculty? |
| Orientation, first-year experience | Learning community or first-year seminar assignments | How does first-year seminar participation relate to ratings of the campus environment? |
| Registrar | Student enrollment, grades, progress toward degree, transcripts | Which engagement activities are correlated with continued enrollment and with academic success? |
| Academic support center | Student use of support services | Do students who visit the writing center report greater deep learning and general education gains? |
| Testing center | Placement test results | How do provisional students rate the campus environment for learning? |
| Athletics | Team participation | Are student athletes less engaged than nonathletes in effective educational practices? |
| Academic departments | Honors programs, capstone courses, portfolios | Do students in selective academic programs participate in more effective educational practices? |
| Student affairs | Cocurricular participation (for example, fraternity or sorority, student government) | Are students who participate in cocurricular activities as engaged in academic learning? |

Table 3.4 lists examples of student records that may be linked with engagement data and suggests questions researchers may ask. Such analyses can also generate discussions that contribute to the development of a culture of evidence. Using multiple sources of data expands the number of questions that institutional researchers can answer for campus assessment, particularly to inform critical programmatic and curricular decisions.

## Working with Multiple Years of Student Engagement Data

To inform institutional improvement efforts, it is best to collect data about student experiences across multiple years. More than three-quarters of NSSE

NEW DIRECTIONS FOR INSTITUTIONAL RESEARCH • DOI: 10.1002/ir

institutions have participated more than once. The UCLA-based Cooperative Institutional Research Programs has hundreds of institutions that have participated annually for decades. As colleges and universities collect multi-year data on student experiences, institutional researchers seek ways to document and record changes, track possible trends, and evaluate specific campus initiatives. In this section, we recommend analytical approaches to multiyear student engagement data, again using NSSE as the primary example.

Multiyear student engagement data can answer many important questions. The arrows in Figure 3.4 represent three scenarios for an institution that collected NSSE data from their first-year and senior students in 2005 and 2008. We call them (A) cohort comparisons, (B) longitudinal analyses, and (C) cross-sectional analyses.

**Cohort Comparisons.** This preferred approach, represented by the arrows labeled A in Figure 3.4, compares the engagement of students in a baseline year with the engagement of students at the same class level in a later year or years. With cohort comparisons, it is assumed that each year's data offer the best estimate of the class-level population of students during that year. Of course, the first-year and senior cohorts include a different sample of students for each year in the data, and the students may differ in their demographic and background characteristics. Analysts can make statistical adjustments for such differences and can help to determine if engagement in educationally effective learning practices during the first-year or the senior-year experience has changed over time.

**Longitudinal Analysis.** Represented by the arrow labeled B in Figure 3.4, longitudinal analysis tracks a panel of students from the first year to the senior year. The advantage of this approach is that unlike the cohort comparisons, one can observe the same students over time, which means that such characteristics as gender, ethnicity, family background, and precollege experiences are constant. Thus, interpretation of results allows the researchers to focus on environmental factors that may influence the nature and frequency of student engagement in various areas.

## Figure 3.4.  Approaches to Multiyear Analysis

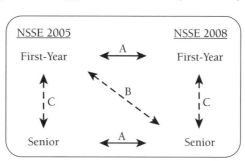

One serious drawback of longitudinal analysis is the inevitable attrition of study participants, which may compromise data quality and limit the conclusions that can be drawn from the data. For various reasons, only a portion of first-year respondents will persist to the senior year, and many of them take different amounts of time to do so. Even those who persist to the senior year may not respond to the survey each year they are invited. In addition, panel data containing only students who entered as first-year students and persisted to the senior year exclude the nonpersisters and the large cohort of transfer students who enrolled after the first year.

**Cross-Sectional Analysis.** Cross-sectional analysis, represented by the arrows labeled C in Figure 3.4, compares the engagement of first-year students and seniors from the same year. For reasons similar to those mentioned above, we generally discourage this approach. Cross-sectional analysis includes both nonpersisters in the first year and transfers in the senior year; thus, the types of students defining each cohort are different. Unlike the longitudinal approach, the cross-sectional analysis attempts to draw conclusions about college impact from two cohorts containing dissimilar students at disparate stages of their college careers.

Another limitation of cross-sectional or longitudinal approaches is introduced when attempting to estimate college impact or value-added by comparing first-year and senior results. This intended purpose is problematic because engagement data represent process indicators, not tests of content acquisition or achievement. As such, a student's engagement score is not necessarily expected to grow or increase from one year to the next, but rather is an estimate of the student's experiences within the context of the courses and campus environment at the time. A host of academic and social variables can affect the quality of student experiences between the first and senior years of college. For example, the first year of college may differ from the senior year in the type of courses students take, class sizes, and the nature of relationships with faculty members. Student living arrangements differ, as do their peer networks, participation in clubs and other activities, and level of intellectual and personal development. Consequently seniors are more likely to interact with faculty members more often about career plans, while first-year students may have more frequent conversations with peers from diverse backgrounds. Ceiling effects may also have a bearing. For example, if the students scored fairly high in a particular area of engagement in both the first year and the senior year, this may be a very positive finding even though negligible differences exist between performance at the two points in time.

Given these considerations, four steps are necessary to analyze multiyear data effectively: (1) identify and focus on specific questions, (2) employ appropriate analytical methods, (3) verify data quality for each year in the analysis, and (4) create a multiyear data file.

First, institutional researchers should identify and focus on specific questions. Multiyear research questions should be specific, answerable, and relevant to pressing campus issues. Tying them to strategic priorities, initia-

NEW DIRECTIONS FOR INSTITUTIONAL RESEARCH • DOI: 10.1002/ir

tives to be evaluated, or policy decisions increases the study's chances of being well received and actually used. The following three research questions represent typical approaches to multiyear analysis:

1. Is the level of academic challenge reported by our students about the same in 2008 as it was in 2006?
2. Given the implementation of initiative X in 2006–2007, how much did our students' level of active and collaborative learning increase from 2006 to 2008?
3. Given several campus initiatives aimed at increasing contact between faculty and students over the past decade, what trends are apparent in the frequency our students have interacted with faculty?

The first question is about stability, which can also be an indicator of data reliability. In the absence of a major campus initiative or shift in the characteristics of the student population, one would expect an institution's student engagement results to be relatively stable from one year to the next. The second question seeks to gauge whether a new program or initiative is associated with higher levels of student engagement. With data collected prior to and after the implementation of an initiative or program on campus, a multiyear analysis can mimic a pretest-posttest research design by comparing engagement levels before and after implementation. Finally, the third question focuses on trends. The number of data points needed for a trend analysis is subjective and in part relies on institutional context and the questions being investigated.

Second, institutional researchers should employ appropriate analytical methods. Once the research questions have been determined, the researcher needs to choose analytical methods that will help identify statistically significant and meaningful changes from year to year. Space allows us only to suggest some ideas in this regard, and not an in-depth discussion or a comprehensive guide for using these procedures. Keep in mind that these methods are not mutually exclusive and can be used together to test year-to-year changes in results.

T-tests are one initial step to determine if statistically significant differences exist and to identify which student experiences may have changed between the years. Although best used with interval-level data, as with NSSE benchmark scores, many use this robust test (and other similar tests) with ordinal-level data.

ANOVA is a good method for reviewing a large number of variables for which three or more years of data exist. A finding of no significant difference between years suggests that student experiences may not have changed across the years. Alternatively, if this test identifies significant differences between years, post hoc tests help identify where changes have occurred.

Regression can also address questions regarding significant changes between years. By dummy-coding the year variable in the model and using the base year as the reference group, one can test for significant differences between the base year and subsequent results. If no statistically significant coefficients emerge, one may conclude that results are unchanged relative to the base year. In addition, assess trends by analyzing the size of the "year" coefficients in sequential order; coefficients may consistently increase from year to year, decrease, or stay stable. Furthermore, using regression analysis with student characteristics as controls provides more detailed information for identifying variables associated with year-to-year changes. Using statistical controls makes it possible to attribute score differences to a campus initiative or policy change rather than shifting student demographics.

Because large sample sizes are often tied to statistical significance even when differences are trivial, effect size estimates reflect practical significance because they indicate the relative magnitude of the difference. For example, Cohen's *d,* the effect size provided on NSSE reports, expresses the mean difference in standard units that can be interpreted regardless of large samples. With regression models, one can standardize dependent variables so that the coefficient of the dummy-coded year variable (as described in the section on regression analysis) can be read as an effect size. Using effect size statistics requires the researcher to establish criteria for determining whether a meaningful change has occurred. The next major section of the chapter has more discussion on this topic.

Analyzing collapsed response percentages by year (see Table 3.1) may make it possible to establish criteria to evaluate whether the percentage change is meaningful. For example, a minimum increase of 5 percent within a two-year period may indicate a real positive change. Because this approach does not test for statistical significance and uses a more subjective evaluation, the researcher may want to take into account sampling error statistics to establish the criteria. The greater the sampling error for each year, the more conservative one should be with establishing criteria for change.

Third, institutional researchers should verify the data quality for each year in the analysis. Reviewing the quality of the data beforehand is especially critical with multiyear studies because each year of data employed contains a certain amount of error. Some survey administrations yield more precise population estimates than others. In some years, the institution may have better data quality due to a higher response rate or because they intentionally oversampled. In other years, there may be student groups that are overrepresented more than others.

Fourth, institutional researchers then create the multiyear data file. Preparing a multiyear data set includes identifying variables that have not changed over the years and merging the cases from all years into a single file. Even minor changes in item wording or the order that items appear on the questionnaire can affect how individuals respond (Sudman, Bradburn, and Schwarz, 1996). NSSE makes available an Excel spreadsheet that tracks every variable by year, detailing whether the item has changed and if it can be compared over time (see www.nsse.iub.edu/html/researchers.cfm and select "NSSE Survey Instruments"). This is especially important if the institution relies solely on the reports generated by NSSE or another provider. If an item has been altered from one year to the next, results for that item on the new report may not be comparable with the same item on the older report. Merging multiyear data can be a tedious job, but doing this carefully will ensure accurate results.

## Putting Results into Context: Interpreting the Effect Size

Earlier we recommended a straightforward way to compare an institution's students with those of a published norm group by computing the Cohen's $d$ effect size. In this section, we address a frequently asked question about how to interpret effect sizes in the context of actual student engagement results. How big an effect is .3 or .6? Intentionally vague about precise cut points and decision rules, Cohen (1988) reluctantly defined effect size as "small, $d = .2$," "medium, $d = .5$," and "large, $d = .8$" and urged researchers to interpret effect size based on the context of the data. Nevertheless, researchers have widely accepted and incorporated Cohen's definition of small, medium, and large into many social science studies.

Cohen described small effects as those that are hardly visible, medium effects as observable and noticeable to the eye of the beholder, and large effects as plainly evident or obvious. In terms of NSSE, the vast majority of effect sizes on its benchmark comparison reports were either trivial (less than .20 in magnitude) or small (.20 to .49 in magnitude) by Cohen's definition.

Following this logic, the NSSE research team considered ways in which benchmark differences would be visible in the data. We compared students attending different sets of institutions according to their performance on the NSSE benchmarks and constructed model comparisons to resemble effect sizes of increasing magnitude. For example, we posited that a small effect size would look like the difference between institutions in the second quartile compared with institutions in the third quartile of the distribution of all institution-level NSSE benchmark scores. Likewise, a medium effect would look like the difference between institutions in the lower half and institutions in the upper half of the distribution. A large effect would be like comparing institutions in the lowest quartile and those in the highest quartile. Finally, a very large effect would resemble the difference between institutions in the top 10 percent and bottom 10 percent.

As a result, the effect sizes for these small, medium, large, and very large model comparisons turned out to be fairly consistent from one benchmark to the next, so we recommended a somewhat finer grained approach to effect size interpretation than Cohen's definition, shown in Table 3.5. Because we based these calculations on benchmark distributions, the new reference values are proposed for NSSE benchmark comparisons and not for individual item mean comparisons. Like Cohen's, one should not interpret

**Table 3.5. Proposed Reference Values for the Interpretation of Effect Sizes from NSSE Benchmark Comparisons**

|  | *Effect Size* |
|---|---|
| Small | .1 |
| Medium | .3 |
| Large | .5 |
| Very large | .7 |

these values as precise cut points, but rather as a coarse set of thresholds or minimum values by which to consider the magnitude of an effect size.

As expected the majority of effect sizes based on these new reference points were trivial (less than .1), small, and medium—a finer distribution within categories from what we saw based on Cohen's definitions. Approximately one-quarter to one-third of all effect sizes appear to be in the trivial range, more than 40 percent are considered small, and the new medium range captures about 20 to 25 percent of all effect sizes. Large and very large effect sizes are relatively rare.

Finally, with effect size analysis, we recommended another important step for putting benchmark comparisons in context: examine individual item responses to see what student behaviors or institutional conditions may be associated with the result. In this instance, looking at the frequency reports can help make benchmark scores and effect sizes more accessible and understandable. For example, many combinations of individual item results can produce a particular effect size. Consider two institutions with the same effect size on a particular benchmark. The first may have large percentage differences on just a few of the benchmark items, while the second could have small percentage differences on all of the items. A series of small differences can accumulate into appreciable effect sizes when combined to form the benchmark score. So looking at the response frequencies of the items within the scale can provide an instructive explanation for a statistical comparison or effect size, which can help administrators and policymakers focus on specific action plans to improve the undergraduate experience. (A more comprehensive discussion of this approach can be found at www.nsse.iub.edu/pdf/effect_size_guide.pdf.)

## Conclusion

Today's higher education environment demands of accountability, transparency, and public reporting are more than enough to keep institutional researchers busy. The widespread use of student experience surveys including NSSE adds another important layer of information about student and institutional performance. While some institutions have not, or may never, use NSSE, almost all likely have information about student experiences, whether from a different nationally published instrument or from a locally developed tool. We hope this chapter provides some constructive ideas to help institutional researchers make the best of student engagement results that campus leaders and others will use to improve the quality of the undergraduate experience.

## References

Agresti, A., and Finlay, B. *Statistical Methods for the Social Sciences*. (3rd ed.) Upper Saddle River, N.J.: Prentice Hall, 1999.

Cohen, J. *Statistical Power Analysis for the Behavioral Sciences*. (2nd ed.) Mahwah, N.J.: Erlbaum, 1988.

Commission on the Future of Higher Education. "A Test of Leadership: Charting the Future of U.S. Higher Education." Washington, D.C.: U.S. Department of Education, 2006. Retrieved Sept. 4, 2008, from http://www.ed.gov/about/bdscomm/list/hied future/reports/final-report.pdf.

Federal Committee on Statistical Methodology. *Measuring and Reporting Sources of Error in Surveys*. Washington, D.C.: U.S. Office of Management and Budget, 2001.

Groves, R. M. "Nonresponse Rates and Nonresponse Bias in Household Surveys." *Public Opinion Quarterly*, 2006, 70(5), 646–675.

Jaccard, J., and Turrisi, R. *Interaction Effects in Multiple Regression*. (2nd ed.) Thousand Oaks, Calif.: Sage, 2003.

Korkmaz, A., and Gonyea, R. M. "The Effect of Precollege Engagement on the Likelihood of Response to the National Survey of Student Engagement." Paper presented at the Annual Forum of the Association for Institutional Research, Seattle, May 2008.

Kuh, G. D. "What We're Learning About Student Engagement from NSSE." *Change*, 2003, 35(2), 24–32.

Kuh, G. D. *High-Impact Educational Practices: What They Are, Who Has Access to Them, and Why They Matter*. Washington, D.C.: Association of American Colleges and Universities, 2008.

McPherson, P., and Shulenburger, D. *Toward a Voluntary System of Accountability Program (VSA) for Public Universities and Colleges*. Washington, D.C.: National Association of State Universities and Land-Grant Colleges, 2006. Retrieved Sept. 27, 2008, from http://www.voluntarysystem.org/docs/background/DiscussionPaper3_Aug06.pdf.

National Survey of Student Engagement. "NSSE 2008 Psychometric Properties." 2008. Retrieved Dec. 1, 2008, from http://www.nsse.iub.edu/2008_Institutional_Report.

National Survey of Student Engagement. *Promoting Engagement for All Students: The Imperative to Look Within*. Bloomington: Center for Postsecondary Research, Indiana University School of Education, 2008.

Nelson Laird, T. F., Garver, A. K., Niskodé-Dossett, A., and Banks, J. V. "The Predictive Validity of a Measure of Deep Approaches to Learning." Paper presented at the Annual Meeting of the Association for the Study of Higher Education, Jacksonville, Fla., Nov. 2008.

Nelson Laird, T. F., Shoup, R., and Kuh, G. D. "Measuring Deep Approaches to Learning Using the National Survey of Student Engagement." Paper presented at the Annual Forum of the Association for Institutional Research, Chicago, May 2006.

Pascarella, E. T., and Terenzini, P. T. *How College Affects Students: A Third Decade of Research*. San Francisco: Jossey-Bass, 2005.

Pike, G. R. "The Dependability of NSSE Scalelets for College- and Department-Level Assessment." *Research in Higher Education,* 2006a, 47(2), 177–195.

Pike, G. R. "The Convergent and Discriminant Validity of NSSE Scalelet Scores." *Journal of College Student Development,* 2006b, 47(5), 551–564.

Salant, P., and Dillman, D. A. *How to Conduct Your Own Survey.* New York: Wiley, 1994.

Sudman, S., Bradburn, N. M., and Schwarz, N. *Thinking About Answers: The Application of Cognitive Processes to Survey Methodology.* San Francisco: Jossey-Bass, 1996.

PU-SHIH DANIEL CHEN *is assistant professor of higher education at the University of North Texas.*

ROBERT M. GONYEA *is associate director of the Center for Postsecondary Research at Indiana University–Bloomington.*

SHIMON A. SARRAF *is a research analyst with the Center for Postsecondary Research at Indiana University–Bloomington.*

ALLISON BRCKALORENZ *is a research analyst with the Center for Postsecondary Research at Indiana University–Bloomington.*

ALI KORKMAZ *is a research analyst with the Center for Postsecondary Research at Indiana University–Bloomington.*

AMBER D. LAMBERT *is a research analyst with the Center for Postsecondary Research at Indiana University–Bloomington.*

RICK SHOUP *is a research analyst with the Center for Postsecondary Research at Indiana University–Bloomington.*

JULIE M. WILLIAMS *is a research analyst with the Center for Postsecondary Research at Indiana University–Bloomington.*

NEW DIRECTIONS FOR INSTITUTIONAL RESEARCH • DOI: 10.1002/ir

4

*Obtaining precollege student data, including attitudes, academic performance, past and expected engagement, and family and student characteristics, is important for institutions to gain a better understanding of the first-year experience.*

# The Role of Precollege Data in Assessing and Understanding Student Engagement in College

*James S. Cole, Marianne Kennedy, Michael Ben-Avie*

Students do not enter college *tabula rasa*. They come with a variety of high school academic experiences, exposure to college information, and family socioeconomic and educational influences, all of which help shape expectations and attitudes of what it is like to be an enrolled college student. Research studies show that high school experiences, engagement, and academic achievement, as well as entering expectations and attitudes, are important predictors of student success. Therefore, to better understand first-year student engagement, it makes sense to consider the backgrounds and precollege characteristics of entering college students.

This chapter has two goals. The first is to clarify conceptually the relationship between precollege characteristics and high school engagement, first-year student engagement expectations, and subsequent first-year engagement and experience. The second is to provide examples of how academic affairs and student affairs use data on precollege student characteristics and student expectations to enhance student learning and personal development. We provide examples from institutions that have used the Beginning College Survey of Student Engagement (BCSSE), the precollege companion to the National Survey of Student Engagement (NSSE).

New Directions for Institutional Research, no. 141, Spring 2009   © Wiley Periodicals, Inc.
Published online in Wiley InterScience (www.interscience.wiley.com) • DOI: 10.1002/ir.286

## Student High School Experiences, Expectations, and Attitudes about College

Many studies show that high school academic achievement and precollege behaviors and attributes are related to behaviors while in college, academic performance, and experiences in college. For instance, Cole and Kinzie (2007) found that 85 percent of the students who reported average grades of B in high school and expected overall grades of B in college actually earned overall grades of B by the end of their first year. In other words, high school grades and grade expectations predicted the first-year grades of many of these students. A number of other studies have also described the relationship of high school and college experiences and academic performance. Murtaugh, Burns, and Schuster (1999) reported that the higher the high school grade point average (GPA), the less likely the student will leave college before earning a degree. Bauer and Liang (2003) found that beyond the traditional predictors of college behaviors, such as high school GPA, standardized test scores, and gender, such personality traits as neuroticism were also important predictors of quality of effort in college, first-year college grades, and performance on a critical thinking exam. In a meta-analysis of 109 studies, Robbins and others (2004) found that socioeconomic status (SES), high school GPA, and ACT or SAT scores were all significant predictors of retention and first-year GPA. Astin and Lee (2003) found that precollege characteristics of hours spent studying in high school, academic ability, leadership ability, and developing a meaningful philosophy of life predict 61 percent of the variance in time spent studying in college. Given these results, these researchers questioned, "How much of the level of engagement observed among students at a given institution should be attributed to institutional policies and practices, and how much should be attributed to the characteristics of the students when they enroll?" (p. 670).

To the extent that an individual has a disposition to be engaged, we should expect a continuity of behavior and experiences between high school and college. Researchers (Ormrod, 2006; Schneider, 1996) define a disposition as an inclination to approach and think about a task and to behave in a particular way. At the same time, past behavior is not a perfect predictor of future behavior. The environment has an important inhibitory or facilitatory role in shaping behavior. From the social-cognitive view, this is referred to as reciprocal causation (Bandura, 1997). According to Bandura (1986), "People are neither driven by inner forces nor automatically shaped and controlled by external stimuli. Rather, human functioning is explained in terms of a model of triadic reciprocity in which behavior, cognitive and other personal factors, and environment events all operate as interacting determinants of each other" (p. 18). What this generally means is that student behaviors, such as interacting with faculty members, and personal factors, like motivation, and environment, such as the climate for learning inside and outside of class, are inextricably linked. In this view, high school engagement is not a disposition but the result of the reciprocal causation between the high school environment, personal characteristics, and the unfolding high school engagement itself over the course of the year. So the fact that high school engagement is often moderately predictive of college engagement does not necessarily represent a student's disposition; rather it represents the interaction of environment and personal characteristics that are often similar in college as in high school.

Of the many personal characteristics students have when they start college, some are for all practical purposes immutable, such as age, gender, and race. Other characteristics are open to influence, such as motivations, expectations, and aspirations, as a result of students interacting with the environment (Pintrich and Schunk, 2002). One such characteristic that has received attention of late are students' expectations regarding their first year of college (Miller, Bender, Schuh, and Associates, 2005).

## What Are Expectations?

Expectations are the result of the interaction of our experiences with our anticipated environment (Olson, Roese, and Zanna, 1996). Expectations may also reflect what we expect to experience based on what others have experienced. In this sense, expectations are based not only on similar direct experiences but also on what we have learned from the experiences of others.

That expectations matter, the central premise for collecting data from students prior to starting fall semester classes, is also grounded in educational research. We have expectations for just about every situation we encounter, regardless of whether the situation is new or very familiar. Imagine, for example, your first day on campus as a first-year college student. Though you have never been a college student, you likely have many expectations about your first year of college. Your probably formed those expectations from your own personal high school experiences in and out of the classroom. For instance, you realize that your shyness to speak up in high school classes will likely still exist during your first year of college. You also believe that your interest in math and chemistry in high school will stay with you in college. Your expectations are formed from the information you glean from others. You create your expectations by talking to others who have attended college, from admissions materials you have received, campus visits, parents, a high school counselor, and others. Collectively all this information leads you to have expectations about your classroom experiences, your levels of engagement, social interactions, and out-of-class experiences during your first year of college.

These expectations also influence the upcoming choices you will make as your first year of college progresses. As Konings, Brand-Gruwel, van Merrienboer, and Broers (2008) claimed, "Expectations affect students' motivation, engagement, and investment of effort in learning" (p. 536). These authors describe three ways that expectations influence our perception, interpretation, and subsequent behavior. First, expectations bias perceptions by directing students' attention to choices that are consistent with the expectations themselves. Second, they bias students' interpretation of events to favor consistency with expectations rather than inconsistency. Third, they bias subsequent behaviors, in that students will tend to engage in a manner consistent with their expectations. In other words, "people tend to behave in such a way that their behavior optimally matches their expectations, and thus, they create what they expect, a phenomena known as a self-fulfilling prophecy" (Konings, et al., p. 536). The idea that student expectations have a confirmation bias that causes individuals to wittingly and unwittingly choose experiences that are likely to confirm their beliefs may explain some research that demonstrates the link joining behaviors in high school, expectations for college, and subsequent behaviors in college (Kirschner, Meester, Middelbeek, and Hermans, 1993; Nickerson, 1998). For instance, Konings, et al. (2008) found that students' expected dissatisfaction with school was highly correlated with their actual dissatisfaction after one and two years in college. Kuh, Gonyea, and Williams (2005) found that many student expectations, including expectations for writing, course learning, and student-faculty interaction, during the first year of college were significantly and moderately correlated with the students' actual experiences in college.

In contrast, many studies have reported that students' expectations are not well aligned with their experiences. The "freshman myth" describes expectations of incoming first-year students that exceed their actual behaviors in college. The result of this misalignment is often increased dissatisfaction with school, decreased academic and social integration, and overall decreased student performance (Braxton, Hossler, and Vesper, 1995; Howard, 2005). For instance, Baker, McNeil, and Siryk (1985) found that the expectations for social and academic adjustment of first-year students at two colleges significantly exceeded their actual reported social and academic adjustment. In a multi-institutional study of first-year students, Braxton, Hossler, and Vesper (1995) found that the more congruent experiences were, the more likely the student was to be satisfied. Level of congruence was also positively related to the likelihood of persisting to graduation.

Overall, research suggests a tendency for continuity between expectations and experiences and a tendency for students to overestimate their expectations in relation to their actual experiences. These results suggest that it is not enough to collect only student expectations data if we want to gain a better understanding of first-year engagement. In the context of reciprocal causation, we also need to know about the personal characteristics of the student and the role of the environment. We know that "expectations are always in flux and continuously revised in the face of new experiences" (Howard, 2005, p. 23). In the first-year student context, these new experiences are the interactions and engagement of the student in and out of the classroom during the course of his or her first year of college. These new experiences can also be thought of as the "environment" in Astin's input-environment-output (I-E-O) model (Astin, 1993).

According to Astin, in order to better understand the impact of college on students, we first need to assess the "inputs," or the relevant characteristics of students on entry to college. The "environment" is the educational experiences of the student: interaction with faculty, peers, and program policies that concern the student experience, for example. The "outcome," or impact, is the result of student inputs mixing with the environment. Because "students generally display a good deal of consistency in their level of academic and nonacademic engagement between high school and college" (Astin and Lee, 2003, p. 669), the I-E-O model helps us to better understand how inputs and environment relate to student outcomes.

The I-E-O model can also help us to make sense of student expectations. In this model, first-year-student expectations can be thought of as inputs in that they are the personal characteristics that students bring with them to campus. However, new experiences (environment) are also influenced by expectations, and therefore expectations continue to change as the year progresses. These environmental factors are largely the result of institutional policies and activities, campus climate, social life, and the classroom and academic environment created by faculty and staff. Therefore, to understand the impact of the environment on the output, we must first understand the inputs and how they relate to the environment.

A model of first-year engagement therefore should recognize the inputs as being both traitlike or stable (gender, race, SES) and situational (for example, high school engagement, college expectations, academic motivation). This parsing of inputs into two types is an important first step before using these variables as controls or covariates in any analysis. Failure to do so can result in the researcher's merely observing spurious correlations: when two variables are correlated as a result of a common cause (Pedhazur, 1997). For example, high school academic engagement is often moderately to highly correlated with first-year academic engagement (Astin and Lee, 2003). However, it may not be that high school engagement causes first-year engagement, but rather that they share some common causal agents. The students' high school engagement is likely "caused" by a mix of dispositions, gender, and other stable characteristics, along with the high school environment. These stable characteristics are also likely to be causal factors in first-year engagement. In other words, some of what causes first-year engagement are the same factors that cause high school engagement. Of course, the environment and other personal factors are different between high school and college. Thus, there is ambiguity as to how colleges affect student engagement on campuses. Expectations can clarify some of this conceptual ambiguity. Given how expectations are grounded in our experiences and influence our perceptions and behaviors, they provide a link between inputs and environment in a way that helps us understand the linkages between past experiences and the interaction with the current environment (Figure 4.1). The proposed model in Figure 4.1 reflects the reciprocal causation of person, environment, and behavior and indicates the I-E-O relationships. It also displays the continuous influence of stable, fixed characteristics of the individual on engagement across time and settings.

## Using Precollege Data to Improve the Student Experience

As institutions of higher education move to expand assessment activities in order to improve students' learning and experiences and to comply with external accountability requirements, the need for more and better student data continues to increase. Assessment is undertaken not only in traditional academic programs, but in institution-wide programs such as general education and first-year experiences (Swing, 2004) and in cocurricular and student services areas (Gordon, Habley, and Associates, 2000). Collecting information from students before starting college, or during the first few weeks of classes, can be a useful source of information for many of these program-level and institution-level assessment efforts. For example, Tinto (1993) stressed the importance of gathering information on entering students in order to assess and understand retention systems adequately (Pascarella, 2001). Precollege information could help us understand the prior educational experiences of entering students as well as their attitudes toward and expectations for their first college year. Precollege assessment data provide important baseline information to document the effectiveness of program-level as well as institutional initiatives.

Many instruments are available to survey students at the beginning of their college experience. A comprehensive database and description of these instruments can be found on the Web site of the National Resource Center for the First-Experience and Students in Transition. Precollege assessments are typically administered during new student orientation or before fall classes begin. Students respond to a myriad of questions about their high school grades, test scores, courses completed, and other important academic indicators of high school success, as well as their involvement in extracurricular activities. Other surveys collect data on students' expectations for engagement during their first year of college, aspirations, motivations, and attitudes regarding academic preparedness. Some of these precollege surveys include the Cooperative Institutional Research Program (CIRP) Freshman Survey coordinated by the Higher Education Research Institute at the University of California at Los Angeles, which has been in use since 1966. More recent additions include the Retention Management System/College Student Inventory published by Noel-Levitz, the Beginning College Survey of Student Engagement (BCSSE), and the College Student Expectations Questionnaire (CSXQ). All of these surveys have companion surveys that can be administered later in the students' academic career.

**Figure 4.1. Model of First-Year Engagement**

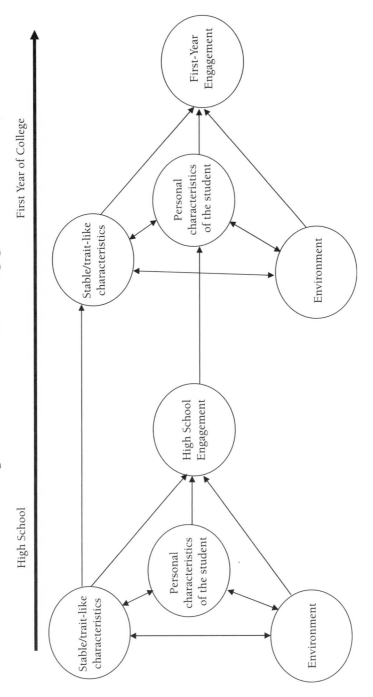

Information gleaned from precollege survey assessments, coupled with students' responses to subsequent surveys administered toward the end of the first year and their academic records, can provide institutions with information about mismatches between their expectations of college, perceptions of their actual experiences, and performance in the classroom. Precollege assessments can supply important information to inform planning processes and baseline data for panel and longitudinal studies. In this section, we discuss and illustrate some ways that these data may be useful to institutions.

**Strategic Planning.** An effective strategic plan reflects consideration of an objective and comprehensive look at the institution's current status. Most planning processes incorporate some variation of an environmental scan, including examination of internal and external forces affecting the university. During the strategic planning process, an institution would benefit from a realistic look at who its current students are, asking whether there are intentional ways in which the institution might want to change the composition of the student body. For example, an institution may seek to expose students to various forms and dimensions of human diversity. Assessing precollege educational experiences and expectations as one part of the environmental scanning process can yield enlightening information about the characteristics of entering students beyond the demographic information typically presented in admissions reports. Subsequent results from precollege assessments can also serve as a metric documenting whether new recruitment and enrollment management initiatives have achieved their targets.

**First-Year Experience Programs.** Many studies have documented the positive effects of first-year experience seminars on college persistence and academic achievement (Pascarella and Terenzini, 2005). In fact, most colleges and universities currently offer some variation of a first-year program to assist students in making a successful transition from high school to college. Meaningful measurement of the impact of first-year experience programs requires the collection of baseline data. Barefoot and others (2005) presented the case studies of thirteen institutions recognized as Institutions of Excellence in the design and implementation of first-year programs. One of the major conclusions of the study was that ongoing assessment was an essential component of excellent first-year programs. Several of the institutions profiled in the study used the precollege CIRP Freshman Survey to better understand who their students were and later used these data in combination with follow-up surveys such as the Your First College Year survey and locally designed instruments as part of program evaluation.

Swing (2004) asserted that students' introduction to assessment early in college may have an impact on the way they regard subsequent assessment activities. Providing feedback to participants about the results of the precollege assessment could have a positive impact on future assessment initiatives. That is, because colleges and universities ask first-year students to participate in other assessment activities during their time in college, engendering in them a feeling that they have a stake in these activities and that their survey results will be used to improve the experience of those who follow them may increase their motivation to complete future surveys. Precollege surveys are tools that can be helpful for both of these functions.

**Faculty Development.** To promote effective learning and employ effective instructional strategies, faculty members need to have an accurate picture of the students they are teaching. In a study of successful college teachers, Bain (2004) concluded that "part of being a good teacher (not all) is knowing that you always have something new to learn—not so much about teaching techniques but about these particular students at this particular time and their particular set of aspirations, confusions, misconceptions, and ignorance" (p. 174). Collecting precollege assessment data as a baseline provides an evidence-based description of the characteristics, perceptions, and expectations of students. Many schools use these data during new-faculty orientations and other faculty development activities in order to help faculty better understand the students they teach. For example, Kalamazoo College offers a workshop for faculty teaching a first-year seminar in which CIRP and other national and locally obtained data provide rich insights into the characteristics of their first-year students. The college used results from this survey to guide discussions about how best to respond to changing student needs and expectations (Barefoot and others, 2005).

**Student Affairs Programs and Related Services.** Astin (1993) pointed out the necessity of focusing on both the cognitive and the affective development of college students. In addition, extensive research (Kuh, 1995; Pascarella and Terenzini, 2005) has documented the benefits of cocurricular and extracurricular activities for college student development. This highlights the need for collaboration between those in student affairs and academic affairs. Precollege assessment can supply a common data set that informs both "sides of the house" about the characteristics of entering students. Student life and residence life professionals, disability resource officers, tutoring center staff, and registrars are potential consumers of these data.

**Outreach and Admissions.** Rigorous academic experiences before college are strongly correlated with success in college; thus, many have called for changes in high school curricula (Kuh, Kinzie, Buckley, Bridges, and Hayek, 2006). Tinto and Pusser (2006) made a number of suggestions to increase student success in college, including establishing linked P–16 systems, creating databases to follow students throughout their education, developing outreach programs for students from underrepresented groups, providing educational development for underprepared students, and "conducting early and continuous evaluation and assessment of student preparation for postsecondary access and success" (p. 20). A number of states have mandated increased alignment between K–12 standards and curricula and higher education to better match colleges' expectations. The report of the Secretary of Education's Commission on the Future of Higher Education, commonly referred to as the Spellings Commission, also recommended that all states provide incentives to institutions of higher education to work actively with K–12 schools in this endeavor. Increased numbers of dual-enrollment programs, early college, advanced placement courses, as well as other collaborative projects are likely to result from this emphasis. Precollege engagement data can be useful not only as a baseline for longitudinal study of the entering students, but in determining whether entering students' characteristics have changed over time. Precollege assessment results can serve as an important tool to set enrollment management goals as well as to ascertain whether those goals have been achieved.

**Academic Advising.** Researchers (Pascarella and Terenzini, 2005) suggest that academic advising plays a role in student persistence and graduation. Effective academic advising involves a teaching component; advisors not only help students decide which courses to take but should help students clarify their educational goals, identify knowledge and skills they will need, and help them reach a realistic understanding of their strengths and weaknesses (Erickson, Peters, and Strommer, 2006). BCSSE results made available to participating institutions include advising reports and individual summaries for each student (identified by student identification number) that can be printed out for advisement purposes. The College Student Expectations Questionnaire also supplies a student advisement reporting option that allows comparison of individual students' responses to those of the institution. These reports offer a wealth of information to start a conversation between advisor and advisee.

**Merging Precollege Data with Other Sources.** Using precollege assessment data to triangulate with other sources of data presents fuller information for data-based decision making and allows campuses to better understand the full experience of their students. These survey data, in combination with academic records of students, can serve as powerful documentation regarding the impact of various institutional programs.

## Institutional Examples

Below are several examples of how institutions have used BCSSE data for advising, faculty development, strategic planning, and other activities.

**Southern Connecticut State University.** One such example of how an institution used precollege assessments for strategic planning, evaluation of first-year experience programs, faculty development, student affairs, and advising is at Southern Connecticut State University (SCSU).

SCSU was one of twenty-eight four-year colleges to participate in the original BCSSE pilot in 2004, and the university now has three years of BCSSE data. The campus community has engaged in an eighteen-month strategic planning process, during which leaders shared data from BCSSE, NSSE, and other sources with the steering committee and many of the work groups assigned to develop specific initiatives. SCSU's new mission statement clearly identifies student success as its top priority, and the vision statement describes the university as a student-centered institution. The campus identified a number of strategic initiatives dealing with student success, including development and implementation of a first-year experience (FYE) program, recruitment and retention of a larger percentage of highly qualified students, and improvement in the undergraduate advisement process.

Use of BCSSE data has been important to SCSU in the development and implementation of its pilot FYE program. SCSU has been following two cohorts of students who entered the university in fall 2004 and fall 2005. With BCSSE scores as the baseline measure, the cohorts consist of students who completed the NSSE during the second semester of their first year. The cohorts are a representative sample of the entering classes.

One of the findings from the study of the first two BCSSE-NSSE cohorts was that students seemed to continue to engage in behaviors that were successful for them in high school. However, these behaviors met only varying levels of success and often simply did not work well in college. For example, a large number of students who reported frequently asking questions in class and contributing to class discussions when they were in high school also reported doing the same in their first year of college. Conversely, students who tended not to ask questions or contribute to class discussions in high school did not do so during their first year at college. While the faculty knew this anecdotally, these data gave them confirmation that a targeted first-year program that would assist students in making a successful transition to college was absolutely crucial for SCSU students. The presentation of this evidence led to discussions about the optimal structure of an FYE program and ultimately to the pilot first-year-seminar program. The university also used BCSSE as a baseline in the subsequent program evaluation of the pilot seminar.

SCSU also used BCSSE and NSSE data for faculty development. Faculty were surprised and disturbed by some of the disconnects between students' expectations of college, as demonstrated by BCSSE results, and their actual first-year experience reported in NSSE results. For example, 59 percent of students in the BCSSE pilot expected to spend eleven to twenty-five hours per seven-day week preparing for class; in actuality, only 39 percent reported doing so in their first year of college. Although many faculty already suspected this, it was shocking to learn that 58 percent reported spending ten hours or less per week on studying.

Students' expectations and reality were more evenly matched in terms of the number of hours per week spent working for pay on or off campus. As part of SCSU's FYE Academy (training for faculty who were instructing seminars in the new pilot FYE program), faculty reviewed and discussed BCSSE (and NSSE) results, giving faculty participants more insight into the high school experiences and college expectations of first-year students. Program organizers asked a panel consisting of upper-class students who attended the discussion to comment on some of the findings. This resulted in a productive, revealing discussion between students and faculty, something that does not happen often enough. Faculty commented that they thought they knew their students, but seeing the data gave them new insight into understanding students' experiences and presented provocative challenges for pedagogy.

By understanding the experiences and expectations of entering students, student affairs staff can better tailor programs and services to the needs and interests of these students. In some cases, this means following up on findings through interviews or focus groups with students. For example, most entering SCSU students reported on the BCSSE that they expected to spend some time participating in cocurricular activities, yet more than half had not done so by the second semester of freshman year as indicated by NSSE results.

SCSU also creates a BCSSE advising report, "Anticipated Difficulties," that has been particularly informative for the advising process in the first-year cohort study. For example, while most students anticipated having difficulty managing their time, students who expected to have difficulty keeping up with schoolwork completed the first year with lower GPAs than other students. In fact, all of the students with GPAs in the lowest quartile expected to have difficulty keeping up with schoolwork. SCSU plans to distribute BCSSE advisement summaries early in the fall semester to first-year-seminar instructors because they are also serving as academic advisors.

**University of Wisconsin–Green Bay.** The University of Wisconsin–Green Bay (UWGB) plans to use precollege assessment data to support the need for its large and dynamic outreach program for middle and high school students called Phuture Phoenix (www.uwgb.edu/phuturephoenix/). The program relies on UWBG peer mentors to develop college awareness and increase educational aspirations in the Green Bay community.

In analyzing its BCSSE data, UWGB found that entering first-year students from the Green Bay Public Schools talked less often with school personnel about their college or career plans, were less certain about whether they will graduate from UWGB and about the highest degree they plan to obtain, and were less sure about what their major will be than all other entering first-year students at UWGB. The mentoring program can target these behaviors. Results from these items in future entering classes can help document the effectiveness of the mentoring program. Program leaders will also use summaries of BCSSE results in the training of student mentors around engagement-related themes, such as, "What does it mean to be a college student?" (with information about time use and important behaviors), and "How is college different from high school?" UWGB also prepares a report on BCSSE results for the campus on student expectations of college compared to their high school experiences and how they perceive college. It disseminates these results to chairpersons, deans, and offices directly involved with student registration and resources.

**University of Maine at Farmington.** University of Maine at Farmington (UMF) is another institution that uses precollege data effectively. By triangulating data from BCSSE, NSSE, and the Faculty Survey of Student Engagement (FSSE), UMF established a baseline for assessing the impact of its shift in 2006–2007 from a three-credit to a four-credit model for full-semester courses. The results from the bundle of student engagement surveys will help UMF identify concerns that may emerge in implementing the four-credit model; administrators will assess the effectiveness of these efforts on the intended outcomes of enhancing academic rigor, raising performance expectations, and involving students in more writing and research.

**Brigham Young University.** Brigham Young University (BYU) compares students' descriptions of their academic experiences from their NSSE results with the expectations they described prior to starting classes on their BCSSE results. FSSE responses make it possible to examine faculty perceptions alongside student experiences. BYU's Faculty Center will report these findings during new-faculty training and internal workshops.

**Illinois State University.** Illinois State University (ISU) plans to draw on BCSSE, NSSE, and FSSE findings to guide campus conversations among current students, prospective students, faculty, student affairs personnel, and other key stakeholders about the differences between the nature of student engagement in high school and what is expected at the university. By integrating faculty perceptions of student engagement into the mix, they hope to understand how engaged learning can be further enhanced through current campus initiatives, such as civic and political engagement, the first-year experience, general education outcomes, and partnerships for student learning. The university will also use the combined data to assess the impact of these and related efforts to increase the quality of the undergraduate experience.

## Conclusion

Precollege student engagement and expectations data are instructive, as illustrated by the examples in this chapter. Specifically, precollege data can be profitably used in these ways:

- Understanding student backgrounds, experiences, and expectations so that institutions can minimize unmet expectations and increase student engagement, learning, satisfaction, and persistence
- Contextualizing strategic plans with entering student characteristics that are relevant for designing effective teaching and learning practices
- Designing and evaluating first-year programs to more effectively align them with student background characteristics and expectations
- Helping faculty better understand who their students are in order to modify curriculum materials and teaching practices
- Informing advisors about students' prior academic and extracurricular experiences, academic preparation, attitudes, and expectations to best advise the student
- Merging with other data sources to provide a richer understanding of the first-year experience

## References

Astin, A. *What Matters in College? Four Critical Years Revisited.* San Francisco: Jossey-Bass, 1993.

Astin, A. W., and Lee, J. J. "How Risky Are One-Shot Cross-Sectional Assessments of Undergraduate Students?" *Research in Higher Education,* 2003, *44*(6), 657–672.

Bain, K. *What the Best College Teachers Do.* Cambridge, Mass.: Harvard University Press, 2004.

Baker, R. W., McNeil, O. V., and Siryk, B. "Expectations and Reality in Freshman Adjustment to College." *Journal of Counseling Psychology,* 1985, *32*(1), 94–103.

Bandura, A. *Social Foundations of Thought and Action: A Social Cognitive Theory.* Upper Saddle River, N.J.: Prentice Hall, 1986.

Bandura, A. *Self-Efficacy: The Exercise of Control.* New York: Freeman, 1997.

Barefoot, B. O., and others. *Achieving and Sustaining Institutional Excellence for the First Year of College.* San Francisco: Jossey-Bass, 2005.

Bauer K. W., and Liang, Q. "The Effect of Personality and Precollege Characteristics on First-Year Activities and Academic Performance." *Journal of College Student Development,* 2003, *44*(3), 277–290.

Braxton, J., Hossler, D., and Vesper, N. "Incorporating College Choice Constructs into Tinto's Model of Student Departure: Fulfillment of Expectations for Institutional Traits and Student Withdrawal Plans." *Research in Higher Education,* 1995, *36*(5), 595–612.

Cole, J. S., and Kinzie, J. "Precollege Student Expectations and Attitudes Regarding Their First-Year of College." Paper presented at the Annual Meeting of the Southern Association for Institutional Research, Little Rock, Ark., Oct. 8, 2007.

Erickson, B. L., Peters, C. B., and Strommer, D. W. *Teaching First-Year College Students.* San Francisco: Jossey-Bass, 2006.

Gordon, V. N., Habley, W. R., and Associates. *Academic Advising: A Comprehensive Handbook.* San Francisco: Jossey-Bass, 2000.

Howard, J. "Why Should We Care About Student Expectations?" In T. E. Miller, B. E. Bender, J. H. Schuh, and Associates (eds.), *Promoting Reasonable Expectations: Aligning Student Views of the College Experience.* San Francisco: Jossey-Bass, 2005.

Kirschner, P., Meester, M., Middelbeek, E., and Hermans, H. "Agreement Between Student Expectations, Experiences, and Actual Objectives of Practicals in the Natural Sciences at the Open University of the Netherlands." *International Journal of Science Education,* 1993, *15*(2), 175–197.

Konings, K. D., Brand-Gruwel, S., van Merrienboer, J.J.G., and Broers, N. J. "Does a New Learning Environment Come Up to Students' Expectations? A Longitudinal Study." *Journal of Educational Psychology,* 2008, *100*(3), 535–548.

Kuh, G. D., Gonyea, R. M., and Williams, J. M. "What Students Expect from College and What They Get." In T. E. Miller, B. E. Bender, J. H. Schuh, and Associates (eds.), *Promoting Reasonable Expectations: Aligning Student Views of the College Experience.* San Francisco: Jossey-Bass, 2005.

Kuh, G. D. "The Other Curriculum: Out-of-Class Experiences Associated with Student Learning and Personal Development." *Journal of Higher Education,* 1995, *66*(2), 123–155.

Kuh, G. D., Kinzie, J., Buckley, J., Bridges, B., and Hayek, J. C. "What Matters to Student Success: A Review of the Literature." Bloomington: Indiana University Center for Postsecondary Research, 2006.

Miller, T. E., Bender, B. E., Schuh, J. H., and Associates (eds.). *Promoting Reasonable Expectations: Aligning Student Views of the College Experience.* San Francisco: Jossey-Bass, 2005.

Murtaugh, P. A., Burns, L. D., and Schuster, J. "Predicting the Retention of University Students." *Research in Higher Education,* 1999, *40*(3), 355–371.

Nickerson, R. S. "Confirmation Bias: A Ubiquitous Phenomenon in Many Guises." *Review of General Psychology,* 1998, *2*(2), 175–220.

Olson, J. M., Roese, N. J., and Zanna, M. P. "Expectancies." In E. T. Higgins and A. W. Kruglanski (eds.), *Social Psychology: Handbook of Basic Principles.* New York: Guilford Press, 1996.

Ormrod, J. E. *Educational Psychology: Developing Learners.* (5th ed.) Upper Saddle River, N.J.: Pearson, 2006.

Pascarella, E. T. "Using Student Self-Reported Gains to Estimate College Impact: A Cautionary Tale." *Journal of College Student Development,* 2001, *42*(5), 488–492.

Pascarella, E. T., and Terenzini, P. T. *How College Affects Students.* San Francisco: Jossey-Bass, 2005.

Pedhazur, E. J. *Multiple Regression in Behavioral Research: Explanation and Prediction.* (3rd ed.) Fort Worth, Tex.: Harcourt Brace, 1997.

Pintrich, P. R., and Schunk, D. H. *Motivation in Education: Theory, Research, and Applications.* (2nd ed.) Upper Saddle River, N.J.: Pearson, 2002.

Robbins, S. B., and others. "Do Psychosocial and Study Skill Factors Predict College Outcomes? A Meta-Analysis." *Psychological Bulletin,* 2004, *130*(2), 216–288.

Schneider, D. J. "Attribution and Social Cognition." In A. M. Colman (ed.), *Companion Encyclopedia of Psychology.* London: Routledge, 1996.

Swing, R. "What's So Special About Assessment in the First Year of College?" *Assessment Update,* 2004, *16*(2), 1–4.

Tinto, V. *Leaving College: Rethinking the Causes and Cures of Student Attrition.* (2nd ed.) Chicago: University of Chicago Press, 1993.

Tinto, V., and Pusser, B. "Moving from Theory to Action: Building a Model of Institutional Action for Student Success." Paper presented at the National Symposium on Postsecondary Student Success, Washington, D.C., Nov. 2006.

JAMES S. COLE *is program manager for the Beginning College Survey of Student Engagement and assistant scientist at the Center for Postsecondary Research at Indiana University–Bloomington.*

MARIANNE KENNEDY *is associate vice president for assessment, planning, and academic programs at Southern Connecticut State University.*

MICHAEL BEN-AVIE *is associate coordinator of assessment and planning at Southern Connecticut State University*

*This chapter discusses four roles—source of data,
audience, data analyst, and beneficiary of assessment
knowledge—faculty can play in the assessment of
student engagement on college and university campuses.*

# Effectively Involving Faculty in the Assessment of Student Engagement

*Thomas F. Nelson Laird, Robert Smallwood,
Amanda Suniti Niskodé-Dossett, Amy K. Garver*

The formal assessment of student engagement, as it has developed in recent years (the National Survey of Student Engagement, NSSE, is one prominent example), is not necessarily a faculty-driven activity. Most faculty members who teach undergraduates are involved in the informal assessment of student engagement by taking attendance, observing student behaviors or expressions in class, providing feedback on assignments, and many other faculty activities involving assessing and making judgments about whether and how students are engaged in their academic work. Furthermore, as advisors, mentors, and concerned community members, faculty also often informally assess students' engagement with the cocurriculum. Yet the formal assessment of student engagement is generally handled by offices of institutional research or assessment offices or is controlled by a department or committee on campus that has assessment of students or student learning as part of its responsibilities.

On many campuses, institutionalizing the assessment of student engagement runs into several forms of faculty "game playing" that Astin (1976, 1993) suggests are common to assessment initiatives. For example, through overcriticism of an assessment process or instrument, faculty members frequently stall or shut down discussion about what can be learned from an assessment project. Faculty members playing such "games" consequently hamper productive use of assessment findings for institutional

NEW DIRECTIONS FOR INSTITUTIONAL RESEARCH, no. 141, Spring 2009 © Wiley Periodicals, Inc.
Published online in Wiley InterScience (www.interscience.wiley.com) • DOI: 10.1002/ir.287

improvement. As a result, those charged with assessment must squarely address a key question: How does a campus effectively involve faculty in the assessment of student engagement to make both the assessment process and undergraduate education better?

Individuals and institutions have tried to answer this question in a number of ways. Drawing on our experiences as participants in institutional and national conversations related to faculty involvement in improving student engagement, this chapter offers perspectives and illustrative examples of ways in which colleges and universities may answer this question. Assuming that the decision to assess student engagement has been made on your campus and that some planning and data collection has begun, we offer several ideas for collecting additional information and meaningfully connecting the collected information to faculty.

We describe four roles faculty can play in an institution's efforts to assess student engagement (see Table 5.1 for a summary). First, because faculty members play an important role in encouraging student engagement, faculty members can serve as a source of data about what they observe their students doing and about their teaching preferences and practices, which can provide valuable information complementary to the student engagement information collected from students. Second, as an audience, faculty members are potential consumers of the findings from any assessment of student engagement. Third, as data analysts, faculty members can be a valuable resource for learning from and disseminating the findings of student engagement assessments. Finally, assessment processes on a campus produce knowledge about what is working and what needs work in undergraduate education. Faculty can be the beneficiaries of assessment knowledge by participating in programs or activities, such as new-faculty orientation pro-

#### Table 5.1. Roles for Faculty in the Assessment of Student Engagement

| Faculty Role | Role Summary |
| --- | --- |
| Source of data | Information can be collected from faculty about their observations of students, the importance they place on aspects of student engagement, and the practices they use to encourage student engagement |
| Audience | Assessment findings should be presented to faculty members through multiple avenues, including reports, meetings, lectures, and workshops |
| Data analyst | Faculty members with expertise in data analysis can assist their institutions through investigations that use assessment data |
| Beneficiary of assessment knowledge | The knowledge derived from assessment processes should be used to inform the development and adaptation of campus programs, including those aimed at improving faculty understanding and instructional practice |

NEW DIRECTIONS FOR INSTITUTIONAL RESEARCH • DOI: 10.1002/ir

grams, faculty development workshops, or department meetings and retreats, that are created or adapted based on what campus community members have learned from assessing student engagement. Before further describing each of the four roles and highlighting what these roles would look like on campus, drawing on examples from institutions across the country, we provide a rationale for involving faculty in institutional efforts to assess student engagement.

## Rationale for Faculty Involvement in the Formal Assessment of Student Engagement

As Kuh pointed out in Chapter One, the logic of student engagement is "deceptively simple" (see also Kuh, 2003): the more students use and participate in effective educational practices—such as working collaboratively with peers in and outside class, interacting with faculty about academic performance and career options, reading and writing at a collegiate level, spending significant time on academic tasks, participating in learning communities or study abroad, and having serious conversations with peers from different backgrounds—the more they will learn and develop during college. This argument gives institutions a straightforward approach to assessing institutional quality. Because the quality of an institution's educational program should be positively related to the amount of time that students are engaged in certain practices, assessing student engagement is a meaningful way to determine how well an institution is doing. Furthermore, since engagement is largely about student behaviors, institutions can readily identify areas where engagement is lacking and focus resources toward improvement.

Perhaps the most deceptive aspect of the student engagement argument is that it makes things seem so straightforward, as if students need only to flip on the engagement switch and the educational light bulb will glow. However, getting students to engage at appropriate levels is not as easy as flipping a switch. Student engagement stems from a complex combination of factors, some squarely attributable to students and others that are the responsibility of institutional actors such as faculty and administrators (Kuh, 2003; Kuh and others, 2005).

How does an institution effectively improve active and collaborative learning on campus? And how does it enhance the ways in which faculty and students interact or increase student participation in high-impact practices like learning communities? Although skeptics may say otherwise, evidence shows that faculty encouragement of student engagement has a meaningful effect on students (Kuh, Nelson Laird, and Umbach, 2004; Umbach and Wawrzynski, 2005). On campuses where faculty members who teach undergraduate courses encourage more active and collaborative learning, for example, students generally engage more in that area. Furthermore, greater emphasis in one area of engagement, like active and collaborative learning, is associated with greater student engagement in multiple areas (such as student-faculty interaction and interactions with diversity) as well as student self-reported gains across a range of academic, personal, and social outcomes. Although this line of research contradicts the common cynical assertion that students generally ignore their instructors, it complements an underlying theme of Kuh and others' (2005) exploration of twenty campuses chosen for their success at promoting student engagement: the success of an institution depends on faculty members, along with administrators of many stripes, being committed to and deeply involved in the improvement of undergraduate education on campus. This means faculty must be involved in the formal as well as the informal assessment of student engagement.

## Roles for Faculty in the Assessment of Student Engagement

We have identified four roles faculty can fulfill. Here, we present a rationale and description for each of these and offer illustrative examples—in many cases drawn from institutions that have participated in NSSE and its related projects—to demonstrate how each role can play out.

**Faculty as a Source of Data.** Most institutions start by collecting engagement-related information from students. For a large number of institutions, part of that data collection is accomplished by using a questionnaire like the NSSE instrument. In presenting the findings to their faculties, campus representatives face an array of responses, some more positive than others. Some faculty members react to assessment findings by reflecting on current practices as well as implementing course or curriculum improvements. Many faculty, however, respond by ignoring or dismissing the findings because of potential problems with the methods of data collection or a lack of trust in the instruments or participants. Others rationalize the findings away or suggest that the results may be valid but simply do not apply to their particular students. While some of this feedback can be useful for institutions as they consider ways to improve their assessment processes, Astin (1976, 1993) points out that this line of thinking and arguing often stalls action and hinders educational improvement.

Collecting student engagement-related information from faculty members is one method institutions use to counter some of these responses. It is more difficult to ignore assessment results when student findings are juxtaposed against responses from faculty members. At the institutional level, the Faculty Survey of Student Engagement (FSSE), and at the classroom level, the Classroom Survey of Student Engagement (CLASSE), are two ways to access information from faculty and pair student and faculty findings.

*Faculty Survey of Student Engagement.* Designed to complement NSSE, FSSE focuses on faculty perceptions of how often students engage in different activities, the importance faculty place on various educational experiences, their expectations for students, their emphases in their courses, and the ways in which they spend time and organize class time. Institutions that participate in FSSE choose between two survey options: whether some of the questions on the survey instrument are course specific or based on faculty members' understandings of the typical students they teach. At institutions using the course-based questions, each faculty member responds to items about student engagement and classroom organization based on a single course taught—the respondent selects a course from those taught in the past academic year. At institutions using the typical student questions, each faculty member responds to items about student engagement based on the typical first-year student or senior taught during the current academic year—faculty who taught more first-year students respond about the typical first-year student and those who taught more seniors respond regarding the typical senior. (For more information about the survey instrument and question options, visit the FSSE Web site: www.fsse.iub.edu.)

FSSE is administered around the same time as NSSE each spring. It is administered online (faculty are recruited by e-mail and complete the instrument through a Web site), and over half of the average institution's faculty usually responds. Institutions have control over which faculty members are invited to participate, but most survey all faculty, all undergraduate teaching faculty, or a random sample of faculty.

By participating in both NSSE and FSSE, institutions can better contextualize their findings or find areas in need of discussion and further exploration. For example, an FSSE participating campus might find that almost 90 percent of their faculty members indicated that student-faculty relationships on campus were positive (faculty are available, helpful, and sympathetic to their students), and about 85 percent of the first-year students and seniors rated their relationships with faculty as positive. Such findings corroborate one another and are consequently more difficult to dismiss. But findings do not always match up. An institution might find that 52 percent of their faculty think it is important that undergraduates work on a research project with a faculty member but only 9 percent of their seniors did so by the spring of their senior year. Discussing whether this level of participation is appropriate given the level of importance placed on the activity by faculty is an opportunity for constructive dialogue about the undergraduate experience on campus.

Similarly, a campus using the course-based questions might find that 29 percent of lower-division faculty (those who respond about a course taught primarily to first- and second-year students) indicated that their course placed substantial—either "quite a bit" or "very much"—emphasis on memorization, but that 63 percent of their first-year students reported that their courses substantially emphasized memorization. Exploring potential explanations of this gap is a productive discussion topic for faculty that connects to issues of course design and student development.

Using the typical student questions, a campus might find that close to 90 percent of their faculty who responded about seniors report that the typical senior frequently—"often" or "very often"—received prompt feed-back from their instructors. However, they might also find that only about 60 percent of seniors report that they frequently received prompt feedback. Such a disconnect in the findings opens the door to conversations about what "prompt" and "feedback" mean, setting clear expectations, and the positive benefits of providing clear, thorough feedback to students. In addi-tion, a result like this suggests that individual faculty might explore how specific aspects of student engagement play out in their own classes, a task that can be aided by the CLASSE, a classroom adaptation of NSSE.

*Classroom Survey of Student Engagement.* In completing the NSSE, stu-dents are asked to report how frequently they engage in various educational practices and activities in all of their classes during the current school year rather than a specific class conducted in a particular term. The CLASSE asks students to report levels of engagement within a specific, designated class rather than across all classes. CLASSE is currently being pilot-tested.

The CLASSE is actually a pair of survey instruments that enables com-parison between faculty values and student behaviors. The CLASSE Faculty assesses which engagement practices faculty particularly value and perceive as important for student success within a designated class. The CLASSE Stu-dent assesses how frequently students report these practices occurring in that class. (For more information about the instruments, see the CLASSE Web site: http://assessment.ua.edu/CLASSE/Overview.htm.) About half of the items on the CLASSE instruments correspond directly to NSSE items. Remaining items address additional variables that contribute to student success such as atten-dance, interest levels, note-taking behaviors, and classroom atmosphere vari-ables. CLASSE administrators encourage faculty members to add up to eight course-specific items that address educational objectives or practices unique to the particular course. This feature enables the CLASSE to be customized to address the variation in educational practices that exist among the humani-ties, the sciences, business, engineering, and other academic disciplines.

Like FSSE, CLASSE is an excellent follow-up tool to the administration of the NSSE. By localizing levels of engagement, institutional leaders are able to more efficiently and effectively target improvement initiatives to address less-than-optimal engagement results. It also enables the leaders to support and reward individual faculty, department, or college-level efforts responsi-ble for the more desirable levels of student engagement that are observed.

In virtually every course in which faculty members administer the CLASSE, there are a small number of engagement practices the faculty member judges to be important that students are not doing or doing at rel-atively low frequency levels. Sometimes faculty know immediately the fac-tors responsible for these disconnects, but more often than not, the disconnects have prompted faculty to think about and ponder what they are doing, or not doing, in class that might be responsible. In addition to such introspections, the faculty members often begin to talk about related best practices with their colleagues, their department chair, and even with campus experts who are knowledgeable about effective instructional strategies. CLASSE results have prompted such dialogue. In the words of one faculty member, "Working on strategies to get students to do more of what I think is important to be successful in my class sounds like a worthwhile objective to me."

What needs to be improved in one class is likely to be quite different in another class. This comes as no surprise to faculty. Not only do CLASSE results vary across faculty but also within the different courses taught by an individual faculty member. That is, what educational practices faculty members perceive to be important in one of their classes may be quite different in another class they teach. This result is consistent with the verbal reports from faculty members who were asked about student engagement results. Faculty frequently remark, "How much collaborative activity I encourage depends on the course," or "I have students give oral presentations in my upper-level course but not my lower-level class," or "I think class discussion is very important in my upper-level capstone course, but only somewhat important in my lower-level introductory course."

Results from the administration of the CLASSE can be used to identify and prioritize areas for faculty development. As one faculty member commented, "If I need to improve in my effectiveness as a teacher, I like working on educational practices that I think are especially important for students to be successful in my courses. . . . I am much more motivated to do so prompted by the CLASSE findings."

**Faculty as an Audience.**  Institutions can present and discuss student engagement findings with their faculty in many ways. The methods for disseminating findings may range from simply copying and distributing reports to more elaborate applications, such as creating customized reports and workshops by department or college. It is important that campus leaders challenge the audience—faculty in this case—not to ignore or simply dismiss the information but rather to be open to its possibilities and give it some credence. Successful faculty involvement promotes discussion of the implications of the findings and results in the development of recommendations or action steps. Findings can be presented in various formats (reports, newsletters, lecture-type presentations, workshops, and retreats, for example) and to many groups (program or department faculty, schools and colleges, task forces, and committees). The following examples provide specific ideas for how campus leaders share engagement findings with their faculty:

Peace College leaders shared NSSE reports with all faculty members each year. The Curricular Issues Committee used the findings as part of the impetus to revise the college's liberal education requirements, with the intention of increasing academic rigor.

Washington State University asked the President's Teaching Academy, a select group of honored faculty, to review NSSE findings and develop ideas for improving the undergraduate experience.

Pace University used a similar approach. At a one-day conference, faculty presented student engagement results and determined additional ways student-faculty contact may be increased.

Leaders at the University of Georgia developed a series of NSSE campus conversations to create an opportunity for numerous campus stakeholders, including deans, departmental faculty, the Student Government Association, academic advisors, members of the Teaching Academy, and the University Curriculum Committee, to get together and discuss NSSE results.

The South Dakota School of Mines and Technology used an internally developed card game with small groups of faculty to disseminate and discuss interesting NSSE and FSSE findings.

Concordia College shares student engagement findings with the campus community through a monthly newsletter developed by the Office of Assessment and Institutional Research. Multiple focus groups of faculty and students also discussed results and presented them to the advisement committee, core committee, and the faculty executive committee.

Hope College implemented a multifaceted approach, including one regular and one extended faculty meeting to address student engagement as well as a workshop that enabled department chairs to share best practices with each other.

**Faculty as Data Analysts.**  When faculty participate in the assessment process, their role is too often limited to consuming rather than supporting the actual analysis of student engagement data. Although it is important for faculty to comprehend what is happening on their campus, institutions may find it even more productive if faculty exercise their analytical skills on the collected student engagement data, especially those who have a particular interest in the scholarship of teaching and learning or experience with quantitative analysis. By inviting faculty to join in as analysts, campuses are likely to benefit from their academic expertise and political influence.

Finding potential analysts might involve recruiting from academic departments or programs where expert knowledge is closely aligned with the assessment needs on the campus. For example, an economist might be well versed in statistics, which could help uncover trends in the data about student-faculty interaction and graduation rates. A sociologist whose research is closely aligned with student activism may help to understand if the campus is a supportive environment for different student groups.

In both cases, campuses could recruit seasoned faculty analysts to join a committee or group that is closely aligned with their expertise or interests and ask them to assist in improving certain effective educational practices. Faculty analysts would work with the committee, likely comprising both faculty and administrators, to better understand the extent to which students are engaging in the assigned effective educational practice. For example, to gain a better sense of active and collaborative learning in general education courses and its relationship with traditional measures of success, a faculty analyst may incorporate student engagement data from NSSE, BCSSE, or FSSE, as well as other institutional data sources. Together the committee and faculty analyst may conduct studies, interpret findings, and make recommendations for teaching practices. If the evidence remains unclear, the committee and faculty analyst have the freedom to negotiate and conduct follow-up analyses or studies.

Whether the faculty member is the person crunching the numbers, she or he is helping to develop the analytical strategy to answer questions necessary for the committee's work. One of the many benefits of having faculty members play this role is their ability to identify limitations in the data while coming up with alternative solutions. This assessment approach is likely to result in defensible recommendations that can garner wide support. Also, other faculty members are less likely to ignore or dismiss the results and recommendations if the faculty members involved in the analyses are well respected in their fields and their areas of expertise are closely aligned with the assigned educational practice.

Another way to incorporate faculty is to find those who are already doing research about student engagement or related teaching and learning practices as part of their academic work and provide them with campus resources to conduct analysis pertinent to their research agenda and campus assessment needs. One benefit to this approach is that the faculty researchers are likely to publish and present findings on campus and elsewhere. Not only do faculty analysts close the assessment loop by recommending implications from their studies, they also educate their campus communities about useful teaching and learning practices.

Besides the obvious benefits for institutions where resources may be limited, recruiting faculty to analyze student engagement data can promote campuswide buy-in, particularly in highly skeptical settings. It may also calm fears about technical issues of reliability and validity if respected faculty vetted the procedures and findings through their guidance or conduct of the work.

**Faculty as Beneficiaries of Assessment Knowledge.** As institutions gain experience in assessing student engagement, campus leaders will accumulate knowledge that can be used to inform faculty development opportunities. For example, centers for teaching and learning often conduct workshops on critical thinking or active learning. Faculty members are the beneficiaries of assessment knowledge when faculty developers base those workshops, at least in part, on campus assessment results.

With an approach like CLASSE, faculty members using the instruments with the assistance of an assessment expert are most likely to gain in assessment knowledge. Based on this knowledge, they build, sometimes with departmental colleagues, strategies and activities geared at understanding and improving their teaching. At times the activity may be as simple as a brainstorming or planning meeting. At other times, it is a facilitated exchange between the faculty member and the assessment expert who has been assisting with the administration of CLASSE geared toward instructional improvement. Faculty members who are involved in these ways find the process much more informative than those surrounding traditional end-of-course evaluations. The opportunities for improvement are not derived by contrasting results between and among faculty, as is typically the case with course evaluations, but by a careful examination of the disconnects between what educational practices the faculty member particularly values in the designated class and what students are doing or not doing.

Campus-level initiatives that benefit faculty often involve the campus teaching center. At Iowa State University, the Center for Excellence in Learning and Teaching used NSSE results to promote pedagogical practices that foster engaged learning at their new faculty orientation, faculty forums, and workshops that occur throughout the year. The Illinois State University (ISU) Center for Teaching, Learning and Technology cosponsored a four-part series, "Improve Student Writing and Still Have a Life." Campus assessment and faculty development professionals built the series using what they had learned from NSSE and FSSE about student and faculty perceptions of writing, as well as their own expertise in the manageable methods faculty can use to improve the quality of student writing in their classes. ISU planned a similar four-part series examining faculty and students' perceptions of the delivery and usefulness of general education.

When successful, these offerings use multiple sources of expertise and knowledge that require partnerships or collaborations between units, such as the teaching and learning center and the institutional research office. Assessment findings ground these initiatives in the particular campus context, help set boundaries for the dialogue, and give faculty a way to gauge resulting proposals and recommendations.

## Conclusion

As Astin (1993) plainly states, "Faculty involvement [in using assessment findings] is necessary for obvious reasons. Any change in the curriculum or in instructional methodology obviously must involve the faculty" (p. 133). However, he also demonstrates that assessment professionals face many challenges in their attempts to involve faculty. Through overquestioning of validity and reliability or other forms of what Astin calls academic game playing, some faculty members, perhaps unintentionally, promote the dismissal and ignoring of assessment findings as well as maintenance of the status quo. If institutions are serious about improving the quality of their undergraduate teaching and learning, they need to find ways to work with, around, and through these challenges. Helping faculty understand and take on complementary roles regarding the assessment of student engagement, as well as demonstrating how they and the institution as a whole benefit from assessment processes, can stimulate the kind of involvement needed to enhance student learning and guide institutional improvement.

NEW DIRECTIONS FOR INSTITUTIONAL RESEARCH • DOI: 10.1002/ir

## References

Astin, A. W. *Academic Gamesmanship: Student-Oriented Change in Higher Education.* Westport, Conn.: Praeger, 1976.

Astin, A. W. *Assessment for Excellence: The Philosophy and Practice of Assessment and Evaluation in Higher Education.* Phoenix, Ariz.: Oryx Press, 1993.

Kuh, G. D. "What We're Learning About Student Engagement from NSSE." *Change,* 2003, *35*(2), 24–32.

Kuh, G. D., and others. *Student Success in College: Creating Conditions That Matter.* San Francisco: Jossey-Bass, 2005.

Kuh, G. D., Nelson Laird, T. F., and Umbach, P. D. "Aligning Faculty Activities and Student Behavior: Realizing the Promise of Greater Expectations." *Liberal Education,* 2004, *90*(4), 24–31.

Umbach, P. D., and Wawrzynski, M. R. "Faculty Do Matter: The Role of College Faculty in Student Learning and Engagement." *Research in Higher Education,* 2005, *46*(2), 153–184.

THOMAS F. NELSON LAIRD *is an assistant professor at Indiana University and project manager for the Faculty Survey of Student Engagement.*

ROBERT SMALLWOOD, *as assistant to the provost for assessment at the University of Alabama, coordinates the development and implementation of institutional initiatives to facilitate student learning.*

AMANDA SUNITI NISKODÉ-DOSSETT *is a doctoral candidate in the Higher Education and Student Affairs program at Indiana University.*

AMY K. GARVER *is a doctoral candidate in the Department of Educational Leadership and Policy Studies at Indiana University and project associate for the Faculty Survey of Student Engagement.*

6

*This chapter suggests ways in which institutions may
implement positive change on their campuses and
addresses the role of institutional research in disseminating NSSE results and partnering with others in
the campus community to use data to inform action.*

# Converting Engagement Results into Action

*Jillian Kinzie, Barbara S. Pennipede*

Assessment information should be actionable (Palomba and Banta, 1999)
in that findings must be used to improve the student experience and educational effectiveness. As Suskie (2004) put it, "If an assessment doesn't help
improve teaching and learning activities, why bother with it?" (p. 18).
Assessment is a worthwhile undertaking when campuses generate meaningful data, thoroughly consider and discuss evidence-based improvement initiatives, and ultimately use results to improve educational effectiveness.

NSSE results are oriented toward such practical use. Each year, more
campuses use their NSSE results in innovative ways to improve the undergraduate experience. Even so, many institutions still seem paralyzed at the
point of taking action on their results. To remedy this situation, in this chapter we highlight the approaches different types of institutions have taken to
move from data to action. These ideas reflect the collective wisdom of several hundred users who shared their strategies and concerns at NSSE user
workshops and also stories from institutional research staff and campus contacts who responded to our requests for information about using NSSE data.
We feature Pace University as an illustrative case for successful use of NSSE
results and mention examples from other institutions. We conclude with
recommendations for gaining traction with NSSE results.

NEW DIRECTIONS FOR INSTITUTIONAL RESEARCH, no. 141, Spring 2009   © Wiley Periodicals, Inc.
Published online in Wiley InterScience (www.interscience.wiley.com) • DOI: 10.1002/ir.288

## Taking Action on Assessment Results

Closing the loop, or using assessment results to improve teaching and learning, is the most difficult step in the assessment cycle (Suskie, 2004). Institutions that have maximized the use and impact of their NSSE results often began planning how they intended to use their results on the day they registered to participate in NSSE. Figure 6.1 presents steps for taking action on student engagement results, which cover three general tasks: (1) planning action before results are delivered, (2) examining and sharing results, and (3) moving beyond NSSE reports by conducting exploratory analyses and collecting additional data that may corroborate or contradict findings.

**Planning Action During the Preresults Phase.** Even before results are delivered to the campus, the first step to use NSSE results effectively is to identify how the content of the survey fits various stakeholders' assessment plans, to remind stakeholders of the rationale for participating in NSSE, and to clarify what the campus hopes to learn from the results. One simple strategy employed to involve stakeholders from the outset is to share information about the student engagement concept and the survey questions well before the survey is administered. Some campuses conduct short presentations at department meetings during the fall term, introduce the concept, and identify questions of specific interest to campus committees or departments.

Illinois State University (ISU) made sure students, administrators, faculty, and staff who had potential interest in the data knew about the NSSE time line and could raise relevant questions in advance. They then tailored workshops to present the results. For example, by sharing first-year student NSSE results with units already invested in the first-year experience, the ISU provost was able to garner greater support for the creation of the Council for the First-Year Experience (CFYE). Campus leaders charged the CFYE with reviewing processes related to the learning and development of first-year students. NSSE results were useful baseline information for the council, and the campus also incorporated them into ISU's Foundations of Excellence self-study project to advance the institution's goals for student learning and success.

Some campuses undertake campaigns to increase campus awareness of NSSE with the specific aim of maximizing student participation in the survey. Western Michigan University's (WMU) Speak Your Mind and Help Improve WMU encourages participation in the survey. Equally important, the campaign promotional materials communicate the value that the campus places on student input: "Your answers will provide a snapshot of the undergraduate experience from a student's perspective and give WMU the opportunity to meet evolving needs." This approach underscores the institution's commitment to soliciting student feedback, In addition, the WMU president has used NSSE to demonstrate publicly the importance of data-informed action and academic and student affairs collaborations to improve the student experience.

New Directions for Institutional Research • DOI: 10.1002/ir

**Figure 6.1. Taking Action on Student Engagement Results**

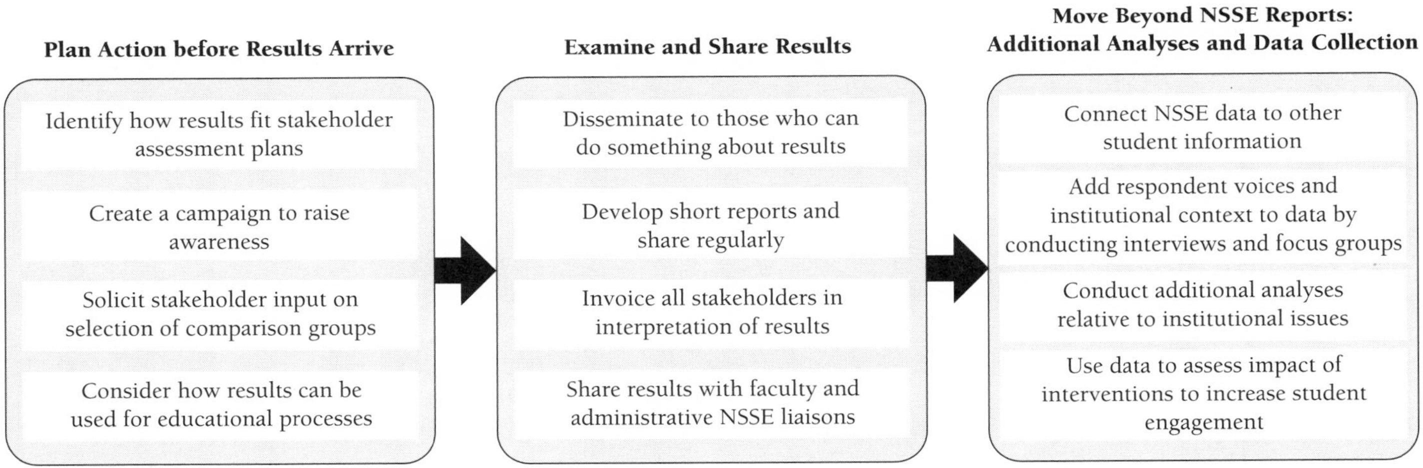

**Plan Action before Results Arrive**

Identify how results fit stakeholder assessment plans

Create a campaign to raise awareness

Solicit stakeholder input on selection of comparison groups

Consider how results can be used for educational processes

**Examine and Share Results**

Disseminate to those who can do something about results

Develop short reports and share regularly

Invoice all stakeholders in interpretation of results

Share results with faculty and administrative NSSE liaisons

**Move Beyond NSSE Reports: Additional Analyses and Data Collection**

Connect NSSE data to other student information

Add respondent voices and institutional context to data by conducting interviews and focus groups

Conduct additional analyses relative to institutional issues

Use data to assess impact of interventions to increase student engagement

Many campuses heighten the interest of academic departments and administrative leadership by soliciting input from various campus stakeholders regarding the selection of institutions for inclusion in their NSSE comparison groups. Texas State University–San Marcos (TSU–San Marcos) circulated the list of current-year NSSE participants to deans, who then selected institutions to include in the university's customized comparison groups. Such customization helps build interest in learning about the results, increasing buy-in for the overall success of the NSSE administration. When NSSE results arrived at TSU–San Marcos, deans and faculty members were already curious about how they performed against their selected comparison groups.

It is also helpful during the preresults phase to think about how to link results to other current or upcoming institutional improvement activities such as curriculum reviews, faculty development initiatives, and program evaluation. Planning this before survey administration allows a campus to consider the value of targeted oversampling or to include grouping variables, such as declared major, grade point average, participation in a learning community, in the population file from which the NSSE sample is drawn. Northern Arizona University's institutional research staff members responded to the interest of the office of residence life in comparing and contrasting the experiences of students in their newly created living-learning center versus more traditional housing. They included learning community students as an NSSE oversample and also used grouping variables to identify nonparticipants so that they could conduct additional analyses. Residence life staff received a customized report that helped evaluate the impact of learning communities on student engagement and are using the results to guide the development of their learning community project.

**Examine and Share Results.** A second step in putting data to use is to disseminate the findings to people who can do something to enhance student engagement. Disseminating data in campus forums, retreats, faculty workshops, first-year experience task forces, and other groups is a productive way to share results. Presenting the data to faculty and staff at retreats before the school year begins can be effective at getting the word out to large numbers of people and stimulate their interest, particularly when the findings are organized around campus themes or concerns. For example, Grand Valley State University presented NSSE results relevant to the institution's Claiming a Liberal Education campus change initiative, which is designed to assess general education gains and align faculty and student expectations with liberal education outcomes, including the extent to which students report higher-order learning experiences and seniors report gains in general education and practical competencies. Similarly, Austin Peay State University emphasized its first-year student data with the university's deans, chairs, and directors, connecting student engagement information with data from the Cooperative Institutional Research Program and Your First College Year survey. Freshman seminars and orientation workshops examined results regarding the quality of the first-year experience to develop and refine first-year student initiatives.

NEW DIRECTIONS FOR INSTITUTIONAL RESEARCH • DOI: 10.1002/ir

Another way to generate interest in NSSE results is to disseminate short topical reports. Miami University (Ohio) created one-page assessment briefs organized around themes, such as Engaging with Other Learners Outside the Classroom. The briefs included results from four NSSE items that asked students to report on the extent to which they engaged in discussions with faculty and others, participated in community-based projects, and worked with classmates outside the classroom. The results were posted to the institutional research Web site, and campus leaders sent them to contacts identified as having an interest in the specific topics. Other campuses share results on small sets of items more regularly by monthly e-newsletters to faculty and staff and all campus committees.

Inviting different groups to interpret the results increases the number of NSSE advocates on campus. Involvement can be formal, such as charging a committee to examine NSSE results or appointing a student group to review results and make recommendations to campus leadership. The faculty and staff committee at Mount St. Mary's University in Maryland charged with examining NSSE results reported on their work to the vice president of academic affairs and all faculty members at an open meeting. One of the follow-up actions was a dinner with senior students to address specific questions and concerns raised by NSSE results as well as discussions with alumni who had graduated five years earlier. During the following academic year, academic departments focused on ways to enhance the rigor of senior-level courses and capstone experiences. Oregon State University appointed students to a blue ribbon committee to interpret NSSE results and make recommendations about improvements in campus life to the vice president for student affairs. William Woods University turned its NSSE data over to students in a market research course so they could use real vs. fictional data to examine quality in undergraduate education. Students interpreted the results and also conducted focus groups to develop a deeper understanding of low scores on items related to the level of academic challenge.

Informal approaches to involving faculty and staff in making meaning of results is also employed at many campuses. The president of Eastern Connecticut State University appeals to faculty members' innate sense of inquiry by sharing results with them and asking them, "Why do you think students say this?" This allowed faculty to contextualize the results so that they could then determine meaningful approaches for addressing shortcomings in the institution's performance.

A more formal, systemic way to involve faculty and staff in using results is to identify faculty and administrative leaders in each college or department to serve as liaisons to the institutional research office regarding NSSE data. The University of Tulsa employs this strategy of identifying faculty champions for NSSE in each college. With the assistance of the institutional research office, faculty liaisons disseminated results in their college and were able to more quickly convince their colleagues of the potential use of the findings as a tool for reflection on pedagogical practice. This approach also worked in student affairs, particularly in admissions and enrollment units that were keenly interested in promoting positive results on the quality of student-faculty interaction as evidence of the university's claims about its distinctive undergraduate education. The institutional research office recognized that the best way to put their NSSE data to use was to identify trained ambassadors who could more easily speak the language and share information within their own departments.

**Moving Beyond NSSE Reports: Additional Analyses and Data Collection.** NSSE results are an actionable and easy-to-read gauge of key indicators of the quality of undergraduate education. For example, the fact that 30 percent of seniors at one institution "never" discussed career plans with a faculty member or advisor, coupled with low senior scores on "acquiring work-related knowledge," points to a possible problem with career planning and preparation. Sharing these results with career services, advising staff, and with academic departments could stimulate discussion. Although many campuses find the descriptive statistics and effect size information adequate for their efforts, many go beyond the standard NSSE reports and use their student-level data file to conduct further analyses and link to student information systems and use their results to demonstrate the need for more in-depth data collection activities.

Connecting student-level NSSE data to other student information can greatly extend the utility of NSSE results. Several institutions linked their student-level retention data to their NSSE results to develop predictive retention models. Georgia Institute of Technology identified several NSSE items as predictors of first-year student persistence: participation in practicum, internship, field experience, co-op experience, or clinical assignment; quality of relationships with peers; the extent to which the institution emphasizes attending campus events and activities; and perception of gains in job- or work-related knowledge and skills (Gordon, Ludlum, and Hoey, 2006). The analysis at Georgia Tech, a technologically based institution with the largest optional co-op program in the nation, illustrates the relationship of distinctive educational practices and student retention and demonstrates the potential for identifying factors associated with student retention that can then be considered in strategies to increase persistence.

Adding respondent voices and institutional context to the interpretation of NSSE results helps make findings more credible and meaningful. When NSSE results are believable to the campus, in that the findings are corroborated by other evidence or are aligned with how the campus is viewed, campus stakeholders generally want more detail. For example, after reviewing students' most and least frequently reported academic activities on NSSE, a team at the University of Wisconsin–Stout commissioned by the University's Teaching and Learning Center (TLC) interviewed Stout students to develop a more contextualized understanding of student engagement. The team asked students about educational practices that students thought were most effective for their learning and development. The TLC staff distilled a short list of effective educational practices from the interviews, particularly around the most important factor to students: the quality of student-faculty relationships. TLC staff circulated these practices and behaviors to faculty and others at TLC faculty development events to increase emphasis in undergraduate courses.

Studies to assess the impact of an intervention to increase student engagement are one way to make the most of results. A small, committed group of faculty teaching the first-year seminar at the University of Wisconsin–Green Bay (UWGB) used their first-year NSSE data to demonstrate the need to modify the content, objectives, and pedagogy of the existing seminar and then to assess the impact of their intervention. UWGB launched a pilot of six new first-year seminars intentionally designed to address shortcomings exposed in their NSSE results. They sought to create a more dynamic learning experience in the first year, include a common exercise project, and more effectively introduce students to UWGB's educational mission of interdisciplinary approaches to problem solving. The faculty leading the pilot designed an assessment project with a pre-post test model to compare levels of student engagement between students in the old versus the new seminars. Assessment results revealed that students in the new seminar course had significantly higher scores across seven key engagement indicators. Persuaded by these results, UWGB administrators decided to double the number of seminar classes and create several new innovative themes. This reform effort was initiated by faculty, supported by institutional research staff, and advanced by UWGB administration and the University of Wisconsin System's Office of Professional and Instructional Development, which encouraged systemic inquiry into student learning. The action taken on results reflects the promise of connecting NSSE to the scholarship of teaching and learning.

Buffalo State College, with support from the Carnegie Scholarship of Teaching and Learning, works with faculty who teach first-year courses to use NSSE results along with classroom-level inquiries into student engagement to make meaningful change in classroom practice. Many campuses have conducted similar teaching and learning inquiries with permission to add NSSE items to end-of-term course evaluations to foster change in pedagogical practice.

## Comprehensive Action to Improve Educational Effectiveness: Pace University

The short institutional examples highlighted in this chapter offer instructive examples for taking action on student engagement results. This section features Pace University's comprehensive, strategic, and integrated approach to using its student engagement data.

**An Overview of NSSE Use at Pace University.** Pace University has participated in NSSE every year since 2002. Its Office of Planning, Assessment, and Institutional Research (OPAIR) spearheads the effort, coordinating the administration, sharing results widely, conducting additional analyses such as examining the experiences of transfer students versus native students, incorporating results into Pace's strategic planning initiatives and accreditation self-study, and assisting the professional schools in using NSSE results for their specialized accreditation efforts.

One of the keys to Pace's effective use of NSSE results is that from the outset, OPAIR initiated discussions with relevant departments and organizations about student engagement and survey results. For example, almost immediately, the OPAIR staff, along with the University Assessment Committee, teamed up with the Pforzheimer Center for Faculty Development and the Center for Teaching, Learning and Technology to consider how student engagement constructs could be incorporated into faculty development programs. Faculty and staff exchanged ideas for best practice based on NSSE results at faculty programs, and interest in results and discussions about effective educational practice has increased each subsequent year.

The campus has shared NSSE results extensively throughout the university community, including the board of trustees, the Presidents' Council and the Management Council, the Provost's Council, and the Deans' Council. The Provost's Colloquia have placed special emphasis on sharing results with the faculty and the university community at large. In addition, after presentations at the various administrative councils, individual deans and department heads requested presentations for their faculty and staff. Thus, each year, a sense of "how we are doing" has grown within the institution. The university incorporated several NSSE items into the assessment of progress in achieving specific goals of its strategic plan. In particular, it placed special emphasis on the goal of student centeredness. Stakeholders adapted NSSE items to fit the goals and objectives of specific programs and initiatives and have used the student engagement data to help measure progress in service-learning, the development of capstone experiences, participation in study abroad, reaffirmation of the institution's commitment to a diverse learning environment, and the increase in positive student self-reports in mastering the learning objectives of the university's 2003 core curriculum. The two examples that follow illustrate how NSSE results can spur institutional improvement.

**Combining Results with Lessons from the Literature to Improve the Sophomore Year.** Pace University has long provided coordinated programs for first-year students to promote their success. These efforts seemed effective, as evidenced by a stable first-year retention rate of 76 to 77 percent. However, there was growing concern about a 9 percent drop in persistence rates at the end of the sophomore year. Motivated by the persistence data and the success of the first-year experience, in the spring of 2004, the Sophomore Working Group, comprising faculty, academic administrators, student advisors, and student affairs professionals, began to focus on developing a special program, or experience, for sophomores. To examine this issue and identify needs of the sophomore population, the group looked to Pace's first-year student NSSE results with the hope that the data could pro-

vide some ideas about what might be incorporated in a sophomore experience. Some results, such as the quality of relationships with faculty, other
students, and administrative personnel and offices, were clues about sophomore student concerns. Pace administrators knew that student problems
existed with office bureaucracy, but it was surprising that relationships with
other students did not receive a higher rating.

In reviewing NSSE results, the Sophomore Working Group wanted to
learn more about these areas where the first-year student experience fell
short. To increase their understanding of these issues and their influence on
sophomore student success, the group read *Visible Solutions for Invisible Students: Helping Sophomores Succeed* (Schreiner and Pattengale, 2000). Group
members quickly made a connection between the factors that were identified with the very real condition known as sophomore slump with NSSE
items that measured those factors. To probe students' NSSE responses and
the degree to which Pace sophomores might be experiencing sophomore
slump, a subgroup of the Sophomore Working Group created a survey that
they administered to the sophomore class. The group gleaned additional
insights from the survey that elaborated the key role that relationships
played in sophomores' assessment of their academic achievements and their
decision to stay at Pace. They also revealed challenges in bureaucratic procedures and the value that students placed on opportunities for co-op
internships and study abroad. The group also conducted focus groups with
sophomore students on each of the undergraduate campuses.

The alignment of sophomore research and further inquiry into NSSE
results discovered through the sophomore survey and sophomore focus
groups led to specific actions and programs:

- The creation and piloting of the Pace Plan, a comprehensive advisement
  model that included both academic and career advisement
- The expansion of faculty mentoring opportunities in the College of Arts
  and Sciences
- Development of a career exploration course intended for undecided
  sophomores and second-semester first-year students
- Establishment of Sophomore Opportunity Day (an all-day celebration of
  sophomores that highlights academic, social, and leadership opportunities for second-year students)
- Installation of a chapter of Lambda Sigma national honor society for
  sophomores
- Officially changing the designation for undecided students from "UND"
  to "EXP" (for "exploring" students)
- Additional outreach to transfer students and greater emphasis on sophomore participation in learning communities and service-learning courses

**Digging Deeper into Data to Study a Campus Concern.** As one component in its assessment activities, OPAIR, along with a faculty member on

the University Assessment Committee, created a research plan to examine the two critical satisfaction questions that NSSE asks of students. The plan called for analyses of NSSE results after three years of data collection, and then again after five years, to identify the relationship between NSSE variables and membership in two groups lying at the ends of the satisfaction continuum: the low-satisfaction group, which included students who rated their entire educational experience as either "poor" or "fair," and those who "definitely" or "probably would not" repeat the experience, and the high-satisfaction group, which included those who rated their entire educational experience as either "good" or "excellent" and those who "probably" or "definitely would" repeat the experience.

At the five-year mark, OPAIR and the university assessment committee analyzed the data to identify five-year trends and engagement activities most strongly correlated with student satisfaction. Although the five-year trend across engagement activities was one of improvement, the percentage of unambiguously satisfied students (those who found the experience satisfactory and would attend the same institution) hovered steadily between 65 and 70 percent. This was in contrast to Pace's Carnegie peers, which consistently demonstrated higher percentages of student satisfaction. The University Assessment Committee was committed to disseminating these findings, and the first stop was with the university leadership. The student satisfaction analysis demonstrated that the aspect of engagement most strongly correlated with student satisfaction was the quality of academic advising ($r = .54$), followed by several other NSSE items related to academic support and the quality of relationships with administrative personnel and offices. Because the administration had imposed a hiring freeze, which included academic advising positions, the Assessment Committee submitted the NSSE analyses to the president and provost, thinking that they might be interested in the satisfaction results as they evaluated the positions affected by the hiring freeze.

The results of the satisfaction analyses were widely disseminated to the deans, allowing them to use the results in setting priorities, and to all members of the President's Council, which included the vice president of student affairs. The next step was to disseminate the results to the entire faculty, inasmuch as most of the thirty-seven engagement activities that correlated positively with student satisfaction were well within the control of faculty. The Assessment Committee thought it was especially important to lead with encouraging results—specifically, the activities that positively influenced students' perceptions of their Pace experience. The Assessment Committee published a newsletter featuring the results of the five-year study and sent it, using the provost's distribution list, to all Pace faculty. As a follow-up, they held a workshop on the satisfaction study at the annual spring Faculty Institute. The wide dissemination of these positive practices, particularly the importance of academic advisement, had an impact on faculty. Faculty were generally supportive of the results because they trusted the multiple time point analysis, and they found that the results corrobo-

New Directions for Institutional Research • DOI: 10.1002/ir

rated some of their perceptions and illuminated their concerns about the quality of advising on campus.

The five-year satisfaction results also fed directly into an issue getting a great deal of attention and concern at Pace: a proposed significant revision in the freshman seminar, UNV 101. UNV 101 is a one-credit course taken on a pass/fail basis by all first-year students. Taught by a teaching team comprised of a Pace faculty member and a student "Peer Advisor", UNV 101 is an in-depth look at Pace University's academic and cultural life, its support network for students, and the services it provides for students. One of the most important changes proposed was to have full-time faculty from each of the schools and the college teach the course. In the past, professional staff and long-time adjunct faculty taught the seminar, along with a handful of full-time faculty. The NSSE student satisfaction results provided additional evidence for the associate provost to convince deans and faculty that the assignment of full-time faculty to UNV 101 would have a significant impact on the first-year experience. A second change in the seminar extended the relationship between the UNV 101 instructor-advisor to a year-long relationship rather than just a fall semester relationship. In addition, the university would assign students to seminar sections based on their professional school or college selection. Hence, not only would these students come in contact with full-time faculty in a meaningful advisory relationship, but they would also come in contact with a faculty member from their school to provide an early connection to their chosen field. With the help of NSSE evidence to strengthen the proposal, fall 2007 UNV 101 sections benefited from the expertise of fifty-seven full-time faculty.

The influence of the five-year NSSE study, as well as the ongoing reporting of annual NSSE results, continues to affect various areas of service delivery at the university. In the five-year study, the item that was fifth in the list of items likely to contribute to student satisfaction was "quality of your relationships with administrative personnel and offices." The administration was already attuned to the need to cut bureaucracy and develop more "one-stop services," and the five-year study reinforced this need. Clearly a positive experience with administrative personnel influenced student satisfaction in a positive way, yet Pace had a history of negative experiences. Student services received additional attention, particularly the registrar, bursar, and financial aid operations. In the previous year, the campus restructured and renamed these as the office of student assistance. A newly hired administrator oversaw the new operation and performed a series of assessments to identify the most pressing problem areas.

As major changes moved forward in the service area, the leadership of Pace University was undergoing change as well. By June 2007, the new president made student satisfaction a high priority and requested additional NSSE studies to better understand Pace's performance over the years. He sent a letter to the board of trustees highlighting Pace's most recent 2007 NSSE results, along with the findings of the five-year study. He extended

Pace's commitment to the improvement of service delivery and has supported formal programs to empower Pace staff to take greater responsibility for resolving student problems.

Improving student perceptions of campus administration at Pace University or other campuses that use NSSE results cannot be attributed to NSSE data alone. However, student engagement data do provide empirical evidence to point to areas where action and change may be needed. Digging deeper into NSSE data by conducting multiyear analyses, and studies of the experiences of different student populations, including transfer students, commuters, and first-generation students, helps institutions get beyond aggregate scores to look more closely at the range of student engagement on campus. Finally, efforts to incorporate NSSE findings in strategic planning, program review, accreditation, and other institutional improvement initiatives connect evidence of engagement to a variety of campus assessment activities.

## Lessons Learned: Taking Action on Results

The examples featured in this chapter demonstrate that many institutions go beyond simply administering NSSE and shelving the results by productively using their student engagement results to improve the undergraduate experience. At the same time, many more institutions could use their results more effectively. Once campuses exhaust all the standard reasons for failing to use data, such as concerns about data quality, dealing with unflattering results, and the need for corroborating data, it is time to take action. The examples described (and many others not featured in this chapter) point to six recommendations for institutional research staff to more effectively use engagement data as a catalyst for action.

**Find Relevancy, and Entice with Results.** Campus stakeholders value and use assessment evidence when it provides answers to meaningful questions and insights into relevant concerns. Thus, sharing NSSE results widely will not by itself lead to action. One institutional research director cautioned, "Don't just send the NSSE report to the deans. Share some results, and schedule a time to meet with deans to get a better feel for challenges they're experiencing, and then hone in on results that can help." Results are more likely to get noticed and then acted on when they are connected to the particular interests of different campus audiences.

**Continuously Disseminate the Data in Small Doses.** NSSE results that matter to campus stakeholders are connected to what they do and when they realize they can do something about the results. At the time of NSSE registration, institutional research staff should consider which stakeholders will be interested in results and how others might be drawn into the findings. Many institutional research offices find it useful to provide brief result teasers to get stakeholders interested in a handful of relevant items. For example, student affairs will be interested in results on the hours students spend in cocurricular activities, the extent to which the environment provides social support, and the extent to which students have had serious conversations with people different from themselves. Regularly disseminate short reports targeted to a particular audience or a specific concern.

**Appoint NSSE Ambassadors.** The more campus representatives who understand the student engagement data, the more likely a campus will use the results. Identifying students and representatives from departments to serve on an NSSE results committee or to be trained on the results so that they can help their peers and colleagues increases the NSSE knowledge base. Faculty representing their particular professional school or college of arts and sciences can act as both a representative of their students' issues in bringing these to the attention of the administration and in return can bring a college or university perspective to their respective schools. Staff members in the institutional research office are in a position to help facilitate this when there is an ongoing relationship with NSSE ambassadors.

**Connect Student Engagement Results to the Study of Real Campus Problems.** NSSE findings have the potential to illuminate a vexing campus challenge to provide evidence of a problem (for example, a lack of opportunity for active learning in the first year of college or underengaged transfer students), or advocate for a particular position on a campus issue, offering perhaps the best opportunity to convert data into action. The way Pace University used its NSSE results to inform decision making during a hiring freeze is one example of applying results to a real campus problem.

**Infuse Data into Continuous Improvement Processes.** While connecting results to campus problems can be propitious, campuses are most likely to use assessment results to enhance educational effectiveness when they are embedded into regular decision making and planning. *Student Success in College* (Kuh and others, 2005), which described a handful of themes shared by twenty "strong-performing" four-year colleges and universities, underscores this approach to continuous improvement. The institutional ethos of continual improvement, labeled "positive restlessness," involves constant adjustment: talking about what works well and what needs to be fixed, monitoring information systems, and maintaining momentum toward positive change. Data aid decision making. Systematically collected information about student and institutional performance validates anecdotes and personal experiences.

**Dig Deeper into Results.** NSSE reports alone should not be used to compel major campus action. As the examples featured in this chapter suggest, results are strengthened when they are corroborated with other data and more in-depth analyses. Focus groups and interviews with students and faculty provide greater insights into findings. Additional analyses such as the multiyear study that Pace University conducted are an instructive illustration. Multiyear studies provide more credibility for the administrative leadership as well as the faculty. Single-year results, though representative of the student population, may not be as convincing as a multiyear study, which reflects the experiences of students over time.

New Directions for Institutional Research • DOI: 10.1002/ir

## Conclusion

While NSSE typically yields actionable results, campuses need other kinds of information about the quality of the undergraduate program to fashion a comprehensive action agenda for the campus. Colleges and universities that couple their NSSE results with data provided by other surveys, outcomes measures, and qualitative assessments develop a solid foundation for taking action on results.

In one sense, NSSE is a checklist of effective educational practices against which institutions can align their particular objectives and goals. These practices represent everyday actions that all administrators, faculty, and student development professionals can understand. Staff members reporting in each of these areas can attach meaning to NSSE results. Initial action does not have to be on an institutional scale in order to be effective and result in improvement. Often the most productive steps occur when one or two administrators, faculty members, or staff members do things that make a difference for the students that they serve. Improvement may begin in small ways but accumulates over time. These small improvements and successes lay the foundation for the larger, more encompassing enhancement plans that grow and spread in the years to come.

## References

Gordon, J., Ludlum, J., and Hoey, J. J. *Validating the National Survey of Student Engagement Against Student Outcomes: Are They Related?* Paper presented at the Forty-Sixth Annual Forum of the Association for Institutional Research, Chicago, May 14–18, 2006. Retrieved Apr. 5, 2007, from http://eric.ed.gov/ERICWebPortal/contentdelivery/servlet/ERICServlet?accno=ED493829.

Kuh, G. D., and others. *Student Success in College: Creating Conditions That Matter.* San Francisco: Jossey-Bass, 2005.

National Survey of Student Engagement. *Student Engagement: Experiences That Matter: Enhancing Student Learning and Success.* Bloomington: Indiana University Center for Postsecondary Research, 2007.

Palomba, C. A., and Banta, T. W. *Assessment Essentials: Planning, Implementing, and Improving Assessment in Higher Education.* San Francisco: Jossey-Bass, 1999.

Schreiner, L. A., and Pattengale, J. (eds.). *Visible Solutions for Invisible Students: Helping Sophomores Succeed.* Columbia: University of South Carolina, National Resource Center for the First-Year Experience and Students in Transition, 2000.

Suskie, L. *Assessing Student Learning: A Common Sense Guide.* Bolton, Mass.: Anker, 2004.

*JILLIAN KINZIE is associate director of the Indiana University Center for Postsecondary Research and the NSSE Institute for Effective Educational Practice.*

*BARBARA S. PENNIPEDE is the assistant vice president of the Office of Planning, Assessment, Research and Academic Budgeting at Pace University.*

7

*After setting forth a vision of accountability rooted in professional responsibility, the author discusses how a substantial number of institutions report their NSSE results publicly, both on their own as well as using mechanisms provided by others.*

# Toward Reflective Accountability: Using NSSE for Accountability and Transparency

*Alexander C. McCormick*

"Demands for accountability by higher education are being heard with increasing frequency." Although this is a familiar thought today, Sally and Richard Zeckhauser of Harvard University penned those words more than thirty years ago in a special issue of *Daedalus* devoted to higher education's "uncertain future" (Zeckhauser and Zeckhauser, 1975, p. 97). Accountability pressures in higher education are not new; they are part of an enduring public policy discourse about the costs and benefits, both individual and social, of higher education. What is relatively new, however, is the prominent place that issues of accountability now occupy on the nation's higher education agenda. A noteworthy example is the 2006 report of the Secretary of Education's Commission on the Future of Higher Education (the so-called Spellings Commission), *A Test of Leadership:* "Colleges and universities must become more transparent about cost, price, and student success outcomes, and must willingly share this information with students and families. . . . This information should be made available to students, and reported publicly in aggregate form to provide consumers and policymakers an accessible, understandable way to measure the relative effectiveness of different colleges and universities" (p. 4).

The Spellings Commission is not solely responsible for the new emphasis on accountability for student outcomes, however. Reforms in the accreditation system also played a role. Accreditation is itself an accountability

NEW DIRECTIONS FOR INSTITUTIONAL RESEARCH, no. 141, Spring 2009 © Wiley Periodicals, Inc.
Published online in Wiley InterScience (www.interscience.wiley.com) • DOI: 10.1002/ir.289

system, though the mechanism for accountability is grounded in peer review rather than public reporting (Burke, 2005). Recent reforms to accreditation have shifted its emphasis away from demonstrating that an institution satisfies minimum capacity and infrastructure standards toward a more explicit focus on an institution's plans and processes for the assessment and improvement of educational effectiveness (Eaton, 2001).

There is an important difference between the visions of accountability articulated by the accrediting agencies and the Spellings Commission. For the accreditors, educational assessment and improvement is an internal matter organized around candid diagnosis and prescription for improvement, and accountability is accomplished through the approval of accrediting bodies, itself the result of an intensive but largely confidential peer review process. For the Spellings Commission, by contrast, the focus is on public disclosure and transparency in the interest of providing consumer information. In this view, accountability is accomplished by the marketplace—that is, the response of students and their parents—which rewards and punishes institutions based on publicly reported performance information (Burke, 2005).

The National Survey of Student Engagement (NSSE), described throughout this volume, has been embraced by a large number of institutions for both internal diagnosis and public reporting. Indeed, the Spellings Commission cited it among four "examples of student learning assessments" (p. 22), and it is one of four possible sources of data on student experiences and perceptions approved for use in the Voluntary System of Accountability (VSA) developed by the American Association of State Colleges and Universities (AASCU) and the National Association of State Universities and Land Grant Colleges (NASULGC). This chapter focuses particularly on how NSSE participation fits in this new accountability landscape.

I begin with a general discussion of accountability and how assessment tools like NSSE offer several ways that institutions can respond to accountability and transparency demands. Next, I review some current examples of the use of NSSE data in accountability and transparency efforts and discuss some important considerations associated with the public reporting of engagement data. The chapter concludes by looking forward: Where might the movement for greater transparency lead higher education?

## Reflective Accountability

First, I want to complicate the notion of accountability. Specifically, I want to distinguish between accountability that is externally motivated and what I call reflective accountability. The conventional understanding of accountability is organized around exchange relations. Higher education is dependent on external actors who control important resources (for example, accreditors, legislators, alumni, prospective students, and parents), and accountability results from demands by those actors for information about

NEW DIRECTIONS FOR INSTITUTIONAL RESEARCH • DOI: 10.1002/ir

organizational performance as a condition of continued access to resources. Because externally motivated accountability is fundamentally coercive, it should not be surprising that it can trigger resistant and defensive responses by those held accountable. Organizations subject to external accountability demands can be expected to attempt to influence the choice or definition of performance metrics on which they will be judged or to challenge the appropriateness or legitimacy of imposed metrics, while these actions will arouse suspicion on the part of accountability agents.

Another factor is the dissemination of performance results. The current national accountability discourse in higher education emphasizes public reporting of assessment results in the interest of transparency. Public reporting of specific performance results may be important to various accountability agents, but it is neither the end point of assessment nor the sole criterion for accountability and transparency. Public reporting demands mean that an organization must not only report specified performance information to a given accountability agent; it also must make those results open to inspection by other parties. This can escalate responses of resistance and defensiveness discussed above.

Reflective accountability, by contrast, is rooted in the professional responsibility of educators and institutional leaders. It is neither a matter of satisfying external constituencies nor imposed by influential outsiders who control important resources. Reflective accountability results from consciousness of and commitment to institutional mission, and the commensurate responsibility to regularly and systematically assess the achievement of core purposes with an eye toward improvement. In this sense, the key "constituent" of reflective accountability is the institution's mission itself, with mission-relevant assessment for improvement as a natural component of the professional responsibility of institutional leadership.

Douglas Bennett, president of Earlham College, makes a similar argument about the relationship between professional responsibility and transparency (Bennett, 2007). He articulates five professional norms that should guide public disclosures:

1. Colleges and universities have a professional obligation to disclose information that is relevant to students making decisions about college choice.
2. Information should be disclosed according to published professional standards and should observe norms of validity, reliability and auditability.
3. An institution's disclosure should include information about student learning.
4. An institution's disclosure should include information about genuinely representative student experiences.
5. An institution's disclosure should include information about the actual prices students (or their families) will pay, and should include information about the likely debt burdens actual students will bear at graduation [pp. 5–6].

Now we will consider the several elements of reflective accountability and their implications. A key element of the literature on assessment and quality improvement is a depiction of the process as a cycle, which typically begins with specification of the information required to assess performance. This is followed by information gathering, analysis and interpretation of the information, and formulation and implementation of an action plan for improvement. Then the cycle repeats (for example, see Maki, 2004, or Chapter Two, this volume). This model of the improvement process can inform the discussion of reflective accountability.

**Interest and Attention.**  At the risk of stating the obvious, interest in and attention to objective performance information is a necessary condition of assessment for improvement. The specification of the information to be gathered as part of the improvement cycle determines the course of organizational learning and improvement. Defining essential performance indicators focuses organizational attention and signals what is important to organizational success.

**Data Relevance, Quality, and Usefulness.**  To yield high-quality, actionable information, data collection motivated by reflective accountability must meaningfully and usefully inform the questions about performance that assessment aims to answer. Relevant questions to ask include the following:

- Is the assessment tool grounded in established knowledge about the topic of interest?
- Will the results provide useful information about factors under the institution's control, and thus subject to intervention?
- If the data are to be based on a sample drawn from a larger population, does the sample design support the planned inferences?
- Do the data meet conventional validity and reliability standards?
- Are the respondents representative of the target population?
- Do the data support comparison of institutional performance against that of peers, against prior performance (or as a baseline for comparing future performance), or both?
- Do the data permit intrainstitutional analyses (say, between institutional units such as schools or colleges or between subpopulations of interest)?

**Analysis.**  Collecting good data is not sufficient to meet the goals of reflective accountability. Institutions must subject the data to rigorous analysis appropriate to the institutional context and the specific assessment agenda. The goal of this analysis is a candid diagnosis of the current state of affairs on campus, with meaningful comparisons to aid in the interpretation of results. What do the data say about institutional performance: how it compares with peers or against an absolute standard, how it varies within the institution, and what the change trajectory is?

**Action.**  This is where the rubber meets the road in reflective accountability. Having identified important assessment topics, gathered meaningful

New Directions for Institutional Research • DOI: 10.1002/ir

data, and analyzed those data in a spirit of candid diagnosis, the institution forms an action plan motivated by professional responsibility to faithfully carry out its mission.

## A Range of Public Reporting Possibilities

While not a required component, public reporting fits quite comfortably with the vision of reflective accountability set out here. The decision to publicize assessment results may depend on an institution's assessment culture and the political and market contexts in which it operates. At the same time, public reporting is not necessarily limited to the reporting of specific assessment results. Indeed, for several components of reflective accountability, opportunities for public reporting exist that can provide meaningful information to institutional stakeholders and demonstrate institutional commitment to excellence and improvement, even in the absence of reporting specific numerical results.

The literature on organizational decision making reminds us that attention is a limited resource (March, 1988). Like other resources, the allocation of attention thus reflects organizational priorities. To the extent that using a particular assessment tool signifies institutional interest in and attention to the subject matter, such as effective educational practices, the simple fact of its use is a meaningful signal to those inside and outside the institution that the subject is important and worthy of systematic inquiry and evaluation. Simply documenting ongoing assessment efforts can demonstrate interest in and attention to the achievement of core purposes.

Using a widely used and highly regarded assessment tool can be an important public demonstration of an institution's commitment to evidence-based assessment and improvement. There is a catch, however, and it is paradoxically related to a tool's wide adoption. As assessments like NSSE gain in acceptance and use, some institutional leaders may be motivated to adopt them more as a matter of compliance or to maintain legitimacy than out of a genuine interest in assessing and improving undergraduate education, though these different motivations are not mutually exclusive (DiMaggio and Powell, 1983). This compliance motivation can complicate the inferences that can be drawn from mere use of a given assessment tool, and they consequently elevate the importance of reporting on what was learned (analysis) and what changes the institution plans to implement (action).

With respect to public reporting of analysis and action, an institution can usefully disclose meaningful information without reporting specific numerical results. For example, an institution can publish and disseminate a report that discusses findings from careful analysis of NSSE data and reports. Such a report can discuss overarching themes—for example, that first-year students are as engaged as their counterparts attending peer institutions, but seniors are somewhat less engaged than seniors at those institutions, or several student populations, including part-time students and transfer entrants, show a need for greater engagement. It can also identify more specific findings—for example, that first-year students exhibit lower levels of student-faculty interaction than their counterparts at peer institutions; senior engineering majors participate in capstone experiences more often than other majors in the sciences; a majority of seniors reported positive relationships with other students and faculty members, but positive relationships with administrative personnel and offices were less common. Even without reporting numerical results, this demonstrates interest in and serious examination of assessment results.

Next, in perhaps the most important public disclosure, an institution can enumerate the concrete, observable, measurable steps it is taking to improve teaching and learning in response to assessment results. An institution that publicly commits to an action plan in response to assessment results not only demonstrates seriousness with respect to evidence-based improvement; it also creates the conditions for evaluating the impact of those interventions in the future. This in turn creates the possibility of collective experimentation. If several colleges and universities confronting common challenges design and test a range of local interventions whose impact will later be evaluated, they can advance the knowledge base to the benefit of all institutions. Such a model of collective experimentation and learning comports well with higher education's commitment to the generation of new knowledge.

While there is considerable value in public reporting without disclosing specific numerical results, the "consumer information" version of public reporting can be even more powerful if specific results are reported, with appropriate guidance for interpretation and interinstitutional comparisons. I will concentrate particularly on the public reporting of student engagement results from NSSE, but the lessons apply equally to other assessment tools.

**Reporting NSSE Results.** Many institutions have made their NSSE results publicly available in some form. Although no hard data are available on the number of institutions that publish their NSSE findings, Google searches on the phrases "NSSE data," "NSSE findings," and "NSSE results" limited to Web addresses in the .edu domain yielded some forty-seven hundred hits after deducting results from selected Indiana University domains that host project-related sites (indiana.edu, iub.edu, and iu.edu; searches conducted May 6, 2008). While more public institutions publish their NSSE results, so do a number of private institutions. Noteworthy examples can be found on the Web sites of Auburn University; California State University, Chico; Elon University; Hampden–Sydney College; Oklahoma State University; and University of Wisconsin–Whitewater.

While publishing NSSE results online certainly qualifies as transparency, it is not the sort of consumer information envisioned by the Spellings Commission, which called for a searchable database containing performance information. Two recent developments come closer to this vision. The two primary national associations representing public four-year colleges and universities, AASCU and NASULGC, have collaborated in designing a model for reporting institutional information using a common template under the VSA. The VSA reporting template, called the College Portrait, contains three sections: consumer information (enrollment, admissions, cost and financial aid, retention and graduation, and so forth), student experiences and perceptions, and student learning outcomes. For the second section, the VSA permits institutions to report data from one of four survey instruments, including NSSE. The template is designed to provide roughly equivalent information from the four sources, categorized as group learning experiences, active learning experiences, experiences with diverse groups of people and ideas, institutional commitment to student learning and success, student interaction with campus faculty and staff, and student satisfaction. Institutions use seniors' responses to twenty-three NSSE items to inform these six areas. Because the VSA strives for content equivalence across different surveys, it offers a sharply pared-down version of each. Thus, NSSE's five benchmarks of effective educational practices, themselves representing a composite of forty-two survey items, are not included in the VSA template, and there is no place to report engagement results of first-year students. As of September 29, 2008, 302 institutions had signed up to participate in the VSA. While the VSA implements a common template, it is not designed as a searchable database permitting interinstitutional or peer group comparisons. (For more information about the VSA, see http://www.voluntarysystem.org.)

In the United States, publishing organizations have been at the forefront of providing consumer information that facilitates interinstitutional comparisons. This group is led by *U.S. News & World Report* and its annual "America's Best Colleges" report. Although *U.S. News* does not include student engagement data in its annual rankings, it has requested results of NSSE participants and published the results from several survey questions for institutions that agreed to share them. More recently, *USA TODAY* began publishing NSSE benchmark data for institutions that elected to release them, making these results available through an online database permitting readers to look up institutions by name, region, or Basic Carnegie Classification. The Web site offers detailed information about the NSSE survey and its five benchmarks of effective educational practice, with guidance on how to interpret the results. For each institution, the five NSSE benchmarks are displayed for first-year and senior students relative to the mean for students attending institutions of the same Carnegie type. There is also a link to the institution's own Web page related to NSSE. There is no overall summary score for the institution, and the site does not provide rank-ordered listings, in accordance with NSSE's policy on the use of student engagement data in rankings. (For more information, see http://www.usatoday.com/news/education/2007–11–04-nsse-how-to_N.htm.)

When this effort began in 2007, about one-quarter of eligible institutions (those that had participated at least once in the last three years) agreed to share their benchmark data with *USA TODAY*. That share rose to about one-third in the months following release. As of May 2008, 391 institutions were participating out of 1,143 that are eligible. At some institutions, information about the USA TODAY program may not have reached the appropriate decision makers. But it is also likely that given the unease and suspicion in higher education about publisher-driven rankings, some institutional leaders were wary of how their data would be used, opting for a wait-and-see approach.

Although the USA TODAY site reports ten benchmark statistics for each institution (five for first-year students and five for seniors), with comparisons by Carnegie class, visitors to the site will observe that for most institutions, institutional benchmark results rarely show much departure from the comparison group mean. This is because institution-level means exclude the bulk of the variation on these measures, which occurs between students within institutions rather than between institutions (Kuh, 2007). This suggests some possible negative consequences of public reporting of institution-level means: it may lead to the mistaken conclusion that student engagement does not vary much, and it may distract attention from where it is most needed: understanding within-institution variation in engagement.

**Considerations for Public Reporting.** The decision to make assessment findings public is complicated, influenced by the institution's assessment culture as well as considerations of audience, information complexity, potential uses and misuses of the information, and the consequences of these uses and misuses. By assessment culture, I mean the degree to which assessment information is routinely gathered, shared, discussed, and acted on within the institution. In the case of student engagement, internal conversations are needed to determine what student engagement means, how it should be assessed, what the results mean, and how the institution should respond. Such conversations play a vital role in helping a campus reach a broad consensus regarding effective educational practices, regardless of plans for public reporting. But these internal conversations also equip faculty and administrators to respond knowledgeably to questions from external constituents regarding publicly reported engagement results.

Understanding and interpreting engagement results appropriately are essential. Even if a campus limits its attention to the five benchmarks of effective educational practice, a considerable amount of interpretive work is required to understand these results: Where does our campus stand relative to various comparison groups, how meaningful are those differences, and what is the trend? How does engagement vary within our student population? Can examination of particular survey items diagnose particular student engagement problems or challenges? Having these discussions is an important exercise, but it is only the beginning, because the surveys contain other valuable information that is not included in the benchmarks. For example, the 2008 edition of the survey contains eighty-five items related to effective educational practice, time allocation, self-reported gains, satisfaction, and background and enrollment characteristics. Indeed, a campus may conclude that several of the nonbenchmark items have particular relevance, such as items related to integrative or reflective learning, satisfaction with academic advising, or self-reported gains. Finally, the accompanying student-level data files allow campuses to link individual students' survey results with other records, such as admissions, financial aid, advising, residence, and registrarial information, permitting more sophisticated analyses that may lead to better understanding of engagement results and better design of interventions.

This complexity suggests the importance of providing context and interpretive assistance to accompany publicly reported results. This is perhaps the most important reason that colleges and universities, and the organizations that represent them, should take leadership in reporting the full range of student engagement results rather than only institution-level summaries. They need to provide external constituents with the essential tools to understand not just average scores but the range of students' experiences. They also need to explain both what these results mean and how institutions are responding. This is important work, because it can prevent improper inferences and inappropriate responses.

Part of the genius of NSSE's design is that the surest way that an institution can teach to the test (act strategically to improve scores) is to ensure that effective educational practices are widespread. But high-stakes uses of engagement data can have unintended consequences and undermine the value and usefulness of the data. If engagement results are directly linked to funding decisions or to institutional rankings, there will be incentives to artificially raise scores. For example, institutional personnel could aggressively promote the survey to more engaged subpopulations, or students themselves could inflate their responses to improve institutional results. Alternatively, some institutions may simply stop collecting student engagement data to avoid negative consequences. Ultimately these outcomes could be detrimental to efforts to improve undergraduate education (McCormick, 2007). The risk of these corrupting influences escalates with the stakes associated with NSSE results. Institutional researchers have a special obligation to act in accordance with the ethical standards promulgated by the Association for Institutional Research (2001) to prevent the manipulation or distortion of assessment results.

## Implications

After several decades, it appears that the discourse on higher education accountability is having an impact, manifested in efforts to gather and publicly report on the quality of undergraduate education. The move to public reporting of performance information is in its infancy, and the uses of and responses to the new information—by legislators, students and parents, alumni, institutional personnel, and publishers—will ultimately determine whether public reporting leads to improvement. Adherence to the principles of reflective accountability set forth in this chapter will help to ensure the linkage between accountability efforts and improvement. The gathering of assessment data should be rooted in a sense of professional responsibility and commitment to institutional mission, and the reporting of results should not be seen as the end point of assessment. Rather, the most important outcome of any assessment exercise is commitment to an action plan rooted in careful analysis of those results. To the extent that public reporting of student engagement results facilitates the effective diagnosis of shortcomings and the formulation of plans for improvement, it can be a positive development. Without appropriate efforts to assist in the interpretation of engagement results, however, public reporting can divert attention away from important findings and courses of action. Ultimately the ability of higher education and its various publics to resist pressures to focus on simplistic comparisons, single metrics of quality, and instrumental interventions intended to affect those metrics rather than the underlying processes they represent will determine whether public reporting serves the purposes of reflective accountability.

## References

Association for Institutional Research. *Code of Ethics for Institutional Research.* Tallahassee, Fla.: Association for Institutional Research, 2001.

Bennett, D. C. *New Approaches to Public Disclosure.* Bedford, Mass.: New England Association of Schools and Colleges, 2007.

Burke, J. C. "The Many Faces of Accountability." In J. C. Burke (ed.), *Achieving Accountability in Higher Education: Balancing Public, Academic, and Market Demands.* San Francisco: Jossey-Bass, 2005.

Commission on the Future of Higher Education. *A Test of Leadership: Charting the Future of U.S. Higher Education.* Washington, D.C.: U.S. Department of Education, 2006.

DiMaggio, P. J., and Powell, W. W. "The Iron Cage Revisited: Institutional Isomorphism and Collective Rationality in Organizational Fields." *American Sociological Review,* 1983, 48(2), 147–160.

Eaton, J. S. "Regional Accreditation Reform: Who Is Served?" *Change,* 2001, 33(2), 38–45.

Kuh, G. D. "Risky Business: Promises and Pitfalls of Institutional Transparency." *Change,* 2007, 39(5), 30–35.

Maki, P. L. *Assessing for Learning: Building a Sustainable Commitment Across the Institution.* Sterling, Va.: Stylus, 2004.

March, J. G. *Decisions and Organizations.* New York: Basil Blackwell, 1988.

McCormick, A. C. "First, Do No Harm." 2007. Retrieved May 6, 2008, from http://www.carnegiefoundation.org/perspectives/sub.asp?key=245&subkey=2349.

Zeckhauser, S., and Zeckhauser, R. "Encouraging Improved Performance in Higher Education." *Daedalus,* Winter 1975, 97–107.

*ALEXANDER C. MCCORMICK directs the National Survey of Student Engagement, housed at the Indiana University Center for Postsecondary Research. He is also an associate professor of education at Indiana University–Bloomington.*

NEW DIRECTIONS FOR INSTITUTIONAL RESEARCH • DOI: 10.1002/ir

8

*Using an organizational intelligence framework, this chapter distills the major themes addressed in this volume: that institutional researchers need essential knowledge about student engagement, ranging from technical know-how, to the how and why of measuring process indicators of student learning and development, to an understanding and appreciation for the reasons that higher education must respond to calls for assessment, accountability, and transparency.*

# NSSE, Organizational Intelligence, and the Institutional Researcher

*Robert M. Gonyea, George D. Kuh*

The chapter authors of this volume demonstrate that student engagement has taken root in the lexicon of institutional researchers and is being used widely in their work. In this chapter, we detail the major themes set out in the previous seven chapters, tying them together using the framework of organizational intelligence (Wilensky, 1969).

In his article about the nature of institutional research, Terenzini (1993) invoked the concept of organizational intelligence, arguing that institutional researchers must be competent in three tiers of intelligence: technical and analytical intelligence, issues intelligence, and contextual intelligence. The framework is interdependent and hierarchical, in that becoming competent in a higher tier necessarily demands competence at the lower levels. That is, before an institutional researcher can possess the knowledge and skills demanded of intelligence issues at tier 2, he or she must first gain conceptual and performance-related intelligences in the technical and analytical aspects of the work represented by tier 1. Here we briefly review the three tiers of organizational intelligence that Terenzini (1993) described and follow each with a discussion about how the current arc of student engagement contains important content and process elements to master within each tier.

## Tier 1: Technical and Analytical Intelligence

The two kinds of intelligence at this level are factual knowledge and analytical skills. Institutional researchers are expected to know and use factual

information about various aspects of the campus: demographic data about students and faculty, including age, race/ethnicity, and full-time or part-time status; program characteristics such as credit hour production; and fundamental rules and formulas for generating student-faculty ratios, grade-point averages, and so forth. Analytical knowledge includes competence in a broad array of methodological skills such as research design, sampling, statistics, measurement, assessment and program evaluation techniques, and qualitative research methods. It also includes the ability to work with large data files and to combine and manipulate them for particular analyses.

The chapter authors have touched on many engagement-related components of technical and analytical intelligence. For example, on the factual side, student engagement introduces new terms and definitions that every institutional researcher should know, including the meaning of engagement itself, the names of the various instruments—National Survey of Student Engagement (NSSE), Faculty Survey of Student Engagement, Beginning College Survey of Student Engagement, and Classroom Survey of Student Engagement—and such phrases as *benchmarks of effective educational practice, deep learning,* and *scalelets.* Yet factual intelligence includes more than just the relevant terms; it also encompasses the data that represent these concepts on their campus. For example, institutional researchers are expected to know based on empirical estimates the various engagement levels of their students. How often do students on the campus meet with their faculty members outside class? How many hours per week do they spend studying and preparing for classes? How does engagement differ by major disciplines on the campus? How many students study abroad, conduct research with a faculty member, or participate in thematic learning communities?

On the analytical side, in Chapter Three, Chen and his colleagues provide helpful suggestions for working with student engagement data, including the use of multiple years of data and the interpretation of effect sizes. The various reports and tools generated by a survey program are helpful only to a point. As several of the authors in this volume urged, institutional researchers must collect data that address questions of concern to their home campuses, for example, the relative engagement of various student subpopulations such as men and women, first-generation students, students participating in learning communities, first-year students living in the residence halls, and seniors by their various major disciplines. Practical tips for working with NSSE data, or any other survey data for that matter, such as dichotomizing items in appropriate ways for cleaner and simplified analysis and reporting or exploring for conditional effects within the data, are also worth exploring. Researchers may have multiple years of NSSE data to examine changes over time or whether scores have remained stable, and also to explore the performance of the various subgroups of students over time.

Terenzini (1993) calls tier 1 intelligence "fundamental and foundational" (p. 4). In terms of student engagement, this may certainly be the case. A basic understanding of the terms and definitions of student engagement, the basics of the survey and measurement of the constructs, and an understanding of how the data are analyzed are important for developing the capacity to acquire the second tier of intelligence: understanding the salient and significant issues surrounding the major decision areas that face campus leaders.

## Tier 2: Issues Intelligence

Issues intelligence refers to understanding the substantive and procedural problems that require the researcher's best technical and analytical intelligence. Substantive issues are important challenges that face the institution and the campus leaders who manage them. For example, the institution needs evidence on how well students are learning, the resources that programs need to function at optimum performance levels, and dimensions of institutional quality that can be documented through accreditation. Procedural issues are about how the human side of the institution functions, such as the informal power structure, reward systems, campus politics, and how to work successfully with people within the system to accomplish goals.

With regard to substantive issues, engagement provides crucial information about the teaching and learning environment on the campus, where resources are well used by students and where they are poorly appointed, and diagnostics about what can be done to improve students' learning experiences. Toward these ends, Cole, Kennedy, and Ben-Avie explain in Chapter Four the importance of obtaining information about students' high school experiences and their expectations for engagement in college. With these data in hand, institutions can better determine how to more effectively allocate resources in the first year, address the particular needs of students, and have a better way to estimate the impact of the campus teaching and learning environment on student outcomes. Banta, Pike, and Hansen discuss in Chapter Two how institutional researchers can use engagement data in assessing student learning outcomes and in accreditation self-studies. At the core of the Indiana University–Purdue University Indianapolis assessment cycle is evidence, one source of which is NSSE. This information has been especially helpful in documenting the value of the campus's learning communities, effectively illustrating how process indicators can be used to assess a program designed to provide a richer learning environment for first-year students.

With regard to procedural issues, two chapters help institutional researchers navigate the informal power structures on campus as they work to maximize the utility of student engagement data. Nelson Laird, Smallwood, Niskodé-Dossett, and Garver offer in Chapter Five a straightforward primer for involving faculty members in assessment. Experienced institutional researchers know too well what happens when faculty members resist efforts to collect and use data for improvement. These authors go beyond clichés about getting faculty buy-in, setting forth four functional and supportive roles that faculty can play in using NSSE results: being a source of data, being an audience, being data analysts, and being the beneficiaries of the data. An institution that strives to reshape its culture into one that values evidence in decision making would do well to promote these roles among the faculty and lead faculty away from the overly critical, dismissing tactics that too often stifle assessment and improvement on our campuses.

In Chapter Six, Kinzie and Pennipede address a form of procedural intelligence as they advise how to turn engagement results into action by understanding how to effectively communicate results to a broad campus audience. Like Banta, Pike, and Hansen, they make plain why assessment efforts must be tailored to the campus context, giving many examples of institutions that apply their engagement data toward real improvements. They recommend planning early, sharing results smartly and widely, and digging deep into the results through additional analysis and corroborating the results with other data on campus. Their six recommendations offer instructive, practical advice to institutional researchers about how to work effectively within the political climate of the campus by keeping the evidence meaningful, disseminating results in small doses, recruiting ambassadors who advocate within their unit, connecting engagement data to real campus problems, embedding the measure of engagement into continuous improvement efforts, and corroborating student engagement results with other data. Ultimately assessment is worth the effort only when it results in real change to programs, policy, or practice and if such changes result in improvements in teaching and learning.

## Tier 3: Contextual Intelligence

Contextual intelligence, the third and most advanced form of organizational intelligence, requires an informed perspective on both the history and culture of higher education and the particular campus where the institutional researcher works. This means institutional researchers must know why the institution was founded and how it responded over the years to the external forces that shaped it. It includes understanding the various campus cultures of faculty, staff, and students, as well as knowledge of local, state, and federal governance issues that define their institution's context for institutional policymaking.

In this vein, Kuh reminds us in Chapter One that the meaning of the engagement concept has evolved over time, from the early time-on-task studies, to quality of effort and involvement theory, to the current broad adoption of the term *student engagement*. He also puts the rapid growth of the NSSE and CCSSE programs in the context of the assessment and accountability movements and the drive to improve teaching and learning in higher education. Indeed, NSSE's three-pronged purpose and philosophy—providing actionable data to institutions, documenting effective educational practices, and public advocacy of engagement as an indicator of institutional quality—came out of the climate of scrutiny that institutions of higher education currently face.

McCormick's discussion in Chapter Seven of the role of student engagement in accountability and public reporting provides additional contextual intelligence to institutional research. As colleges and universities experiment with ways to appropriately communicate indicators of institutional quality to the public, McCormick encourages institutions to use assessment efforts not merely to show positive results, but also to identify areas where the institution falls short of its potential and where it may enhance the student experience. While reporting results is a key part of the assessment cycle, campuses must put the results to instructive ends to close the loop. This requires putting in motion an action plan to continuously improve teaching and learning and other aspects of student and institutional performance. McCormick's set of principles for reflective accountability, beginning with professional responsibility and commitment to institutional mission, calls on researchers to know their institutions well enough to respond to the public calls for transparency with high-quality information presented with integrity.

## Conclusion

Terenzini's (1993) description of organizational intelligence as applied to institutional research served as a useful frame to synthesize many of the key points made by the contributors to this volume. They call for institutional researchers to become knowledgeable about student engagement on all three levels of intelligence: technical and analytical, issues, and contextual.

Institutional researchers with a capacity for organizational intelligence will be able to adapt to ways the student engagement construct and its uses may evolve in the future. Certainly new understandings and approaches will emerge that will improve or supplant existing notions of student engagement. We may discover new forms of engagement that are equally relevant and influential aspects of the student learning process and can be effectively used as indicators of institutional quality. Certainly researchers may discover more effective ways to combine data for more powerful analysis.

Several challenges must be addressed to move forward. Research is needed to learn more about the complex relationships between student engagement and outcomes, dissecting which forms of engagement are most effective for different types of outcomes and different groups of students. Recent studies have shown encouraging results along these lines, including the Connecting the Dots study (Kuh and others, 2008) and the Wabash National Study of Liberal Arts Education (Pascarella, Seifert, and Blaich, 2008). What is more, many individual institutions report positive findings each year to NSSE that are reported in the annual reports available on the NSSE Web site (www.nsse.iub.edu/html/annual_reports. cfm). Institutional researchers are encouraged to continue to link engagement data to outcomes and test for changes in terms of teaching and learning approaches and student learning.

Changing technology will also affect our ability to collect data from students. When NSSE was launched in 2000, 39 percent of the students completed the survey online. In 2008 nearly all students—96 percent —completed the Web version. Online surveys have become inexpensive ways to collect data, but the proliferation of questionnaires on campuses and response rates trending downward points to the likelihood of survey fatigue. Engagement surveys are but one type of assessment measures that must fit into an ever crowding demand for information from students for assessment.

Assessment activities are increasingly decentralized and conducted at the unit or departmental level (Muffo, 2001) so that the results can be used more readily by faculty and staff who are in a position to modify their policies and practices to improve student learning. Campus strategies are thus becoming more complex as assessments are tailored to disciplinary units, programs, general education, student affairs functional units, and evaluation of funded projects: learning communities, alternative residence hall arrangements, and so on. This trend is responding to the need for more meaningful data closer to the point where students engage with the campus, but it also creates more data and more administrative challenges for time- and resource-strapped institutional research offices. At the same time, they must help educate campus leaders and the public about what engagement data represent—the conditions that foster learning and not learning outcomes themselves—and how to responsibly use engagement data (Kuh, 2007).

In conclusion, institutional researchers who work with student engagement data must possess intelligence ranging from technical know-how, to the how and why of measuring process indicators of student learning and development, to the historic and cultural issues facing higher education with regard to assessment and accountability. As the engagement construct continues to evolve, the field of institutional research must continue to be prepared with the essential knowledge of the domain and incorporate it in their ongoing efforts to provide accurate, actionable data for institutional accountability and to guide improvement efforts.

## References

Kuh, G. D. "Risky Business: Promises and Pitfalls of Institutional Transparency." *Change*, 2007, *39*(5), 30–35.

Kuh, G. D., and others. "Unmasking the Effects of Student Engagement on College Grades and Persistence." *Journal of Higher Education*, 2008, *79*, 540–563.

Muffo, J. "Institutional Effectiveness, Student Learning, and Outcomes Assessment." In R. D. Howard (ed.), *Institutional Research: Decision Support in Higher Education*. Tallahassee, Fla.: Association for Institutional Research, 2001.

Pascarella, E. T., Seifert, T. A., and Blaich, C. "Validation of the NSSE Benchmarks Against Liberal Arts Outcomes." Paper presented at the annual conference of the Association for the Study of Higher Education, Jacksonville, Fla., Nov. 2008.

Terenzini, P. "On the Nature of Institutional Research and the Knowledge and Skills It Requires." *Research in Higher Education,* 1993, 34(1), 1–10.

Wilensky, H. L. *Organizational Intelligence: Knowledge and Policy in Government and Industry.* New York: Basic Books, 1969.

ROBERT M. GONYEA *is associate director of the Center for Postsecondary Research at Indiana University–Bloomington.*

GEORGE D. KUH *is Chancellor's Professor of Higher Education and director of the Center for Postsecondary Research at Indiana University–Bloomington.*

# INDEX

be thrown out of court if it fails to meet the rules of evidence or contradicts current legal standing. The information contained within this volume will benefit institutional research practitioners and contribute to a more frequent dialogue concerning the complexities of statistical science within the legal environment.
ISBN: 978-04703-97619

IR137    **Alternative Perspectives in Institutional Planning**
*Terry T. Ishitani*
Institutional planning is coming to the fore in higher education as states, the federal government, and the public increasingly demand accountability. Institutional researchers, the data stewards for colleges and universities, are becoming involved in such strategic planning, supporting efforts to strengthen institutional efficiency and effectiveness in policymaking. Researchers find that locating, preparing, and presenting necessary data and information for planners is a challenging exercise. In this volume of *New Directions for Institutional Research*, administrators, consultants, researchers, and scholars provide unique, innovative approaches to that challenge. Some authors introduce program applications and statistical techniques; others share case studies. The variety of perspectives and depths of focus makes this a timely, useful guide for institutional researchers.
ISBN: 978-04703-84534

IR136    **Using Qualitative Methods in Institutional Assessment**
*Shaun R. Harper, Samuel D. Museus*
This volume of *New Directions for Institutional Research* advocates the broad use of qualitative methods in assessment across American higher education: campus cultures, academic success and retention programs, student experiences and learning, and teaching effectiveness. The chapter authors suggest that responses to demands for increased accountability will be insufficient if researchers continue to rely almost exclusively on statistical analyses to assess institutional effectiveness. Instead, they recommend a variety of qualitative approaches that can produce rich and instructive data to guide institutional decision-making and action. In addition, they dispel common myths and misconceptions regarding the use of qualitative methods in assessment.
ISBN: 978-04702-83615

IR135    **Space: The Final Frontier for Institutional Research**
*Nicholas A. Valcik*
Facilities information, once a world of precious drawings and laborious calculations, has been transformed by the power of information technology. Blueprints securely locked in cabinets have given way to online systems based on geospatial information systems (GIS). The result is nimble systems adaptable to purposes across administrations, applications that integrate divisions—business, institutional research, student affairs—with shared information. This volume of *New Directions for Institutional Research* delves into this new world of facilities information. The authors show how to gather data and how state and other agencies use it. They discuss the necessity of accurate, accessible information for determining and apportioning indirect costs. They look at its use for student recruitment and retention, and they demonstrate how it can even be used to correlate various classroom attributes with student learning success. With twenty-first-century technology, facilities data is useful far beyond traditional business affairs operations—it has become integral to institutional planning and operation.
ISBN: 978-04702-55254

review prior research and best practices, then investigate new approaches to assessment, action research, action inquiry, and evaluation. Lessons learned can inform strategies of administrators, faculty, and everyone interested in improving success for all students.
ISBN: 0-7879-8759-X

IR129    **Analyzing Faculty Work and Rewards: Using Boyer's Four Domains of Scholarship**
*John M. Braxton*
Boyer's four domains—scholarships of discovery, application, integration, and teaching—influence and define scholars as their professional roles, career stages, and research goals change. This volume offers practical suggestions for academic reward structure, graduate school preparation, and state policy.
ISBN: 0-7879-8674-7

IR128    **Workforce Development and Higher Education: A Strategic Role for Institutional Research**
*Richard A. Voorhees, Lee Harvey*
Workforce development is a growing area for higher education. This volume examines its conceptual underpinnings from an international perspective, and it provides practical institutional case studies and specific techniques for gauging the market potential for new instructional programs. It discusses suggested projects and studies for IR personnel to consider on their campuses.
ISBN: 0-7879-8365-9

IR127    **Survey Research: Emerging Issues**
*Paul D. Umbach*
Demands for accountability are forcing colleges and universities to conduct more high-quality surveys to gauge institutional effectiveness. New technologies are improving survey implementation as well as researchers' ability to effectively analyze data. This volume examines these emerging issues in a rapidly changing environment and highlights lessons learned from past research.
ISBN: 0-7879-8329-2

IR126    **Enhancing Alumni Research: European and American Perspectives**
*David J. Weerts, Javier Vidal*
The increasing globalization of higher education has made it easy to compare problems, goals, and tools associated with conducting alumni research worldwide. This research is also being used to learn about the impact, purposes, and successes of higher education. This volume will help institutional leaders use alumni research to respond to the increasing demands of state officials, accrediting agencies, employers, prospective students, parents, and the general public.
ISBN: 0-7879-8228-8

IR125    **Minority Retention: What Works?**
*Gerald H. Gaither*
Examines some of the best policies, practices, and procedures to achieve greater diversity and access, while controlling costs and maintaining quality. Looks at institutions that are majority-serving, tribal, Hispanic-serving, and historically black. Emphasizes that the key to retention is in the professional commitment of faculty and staff to student-centered efforts, and includes practical ideas adaptable to different institutional goals.
ISBN: 0-7879-7974-0

**IR124    Unique Campus Contexts: Insights for Research and Assessment**
*Jason E. Lane, M. Christopher Brown II*
Summarizes what we know about professional schools, transnational campuses, proprietary schools, religious institutions, and corporate universities. As more students take advantage of these specialized educational environments, conducting meaningful research becomes a challenge. The authors argue for the importance of educational context and debunk the one-size-fits-all approach to assessment, evaluation, and research. Effective institutional measures of inquiry, benchmarks, and indicators must be congruent with the mission, population, and function of each unique campus context.
ISBN: 0-7879-7973-2

**IR123    Successful Strategic Planning**
*Michael J. Dooris, John M. Kelley, James F. Trainer*
Explains the value of strategic planning in higher education to improve conditions and meet missions (hiring better faculty, recruiting stronger students, upgrading facilities, improving programs, acquiring resources), and what planning tools and methodologies have been used at various campuses. Goes beyond the activity of planning to investigate successful ways to implement and infuse strategic plans throughout the organization. Case studies from various campuses show different ways to achieve success.
ISBN: 0-7879-7792-6

**IR122    Assessing Character Outcomes in College**
*Jon C. Dalton, Terrence R. Russell, Sally Kline*
Examines several perspectives on the role of higher education in developing students' character, and illustrates approaches to defining and assessing character outcomes. Moral, civic, ethical, and spiritual development are key aspects of students' growth and experience in college, so how can educators encourage good values and assess their impact?
ISBN: 0-7879-7791-8

**IR121    Overcoming Survey Research Problems**
*Stephen R. Porter*
As demand for survey research has increased, survey response rates have decreased. This volume examines an array of survey research problems and best practices, from both the literature and field practitioners, to provide solutions to increase response rates while controlling costs. Discusses administering longitudinal studies, doing surveys on sensitive topics such as student drug and alcohol use, and using new technologies for survey administration.
ISBN: 0-7879-7477-3

**IR120    Using Geographic Information Systems in Institutional Research**
*Daniel Teodorescu*
Exploring the potential of geographic information systems (GIS) applications in higher education administration, this issue introduces IR professionals and campus administrators to a powerful presentation and analysis tool. Chapters explore the benefits of working with the spatial component of data in recruitment, admissions, facilities, alumni development, and other areas, with examples of actual GIS applications from several higher education institutions.
ISBN: 0-7879-7281-9

**IR119    Maximizing Revenue in Higher Education**
*F. King Alexander, Ronald G. Ehrenberg*
This volume presents edited versions of some of the best articles from a forum on institutional revenue generation sponsored by the Cornell Higher Education

Research Institute. The chapters provide different perspectives on revenue generation and how institutions are struggling to find an appropriate balance between meeting public expectations and maximizing private market forces. The insights provided about options and alternatives will enable campus leaders, institutional researchers, and policymakers to better understand evolving patterns in public and private revenue reliance.
ISBN: 0-7879-7221-5

IR118    **Studying Diverse Institutions: Contexts, Challenges, and Considerations**
*M. Christopher Brown II, Jason E. Lane*
This volume examines the contextual and methodological issues pertaining to studying diverse institutions (including women's colleges, tribal colleges, and military academies), and provides effective and useful approaches for higher education administrators, institutional researchers and planners, policymakers, and faculty seeking to better understand students in postsecondary education. It also offers guidelines to asking the right research questions, employing the appropriate research design and methods, and analyzing the data with respect to the unique institutional contexts.
ISBN: 0-7879-6990-7

IR117    **Unresolved Issues in Conducting Salary-Equity Studies**
*Robert K. Toutkoushian*
Chapters discuss the issues surrounding how to use faculty rank, seniority, and experience as control variables in salary-equity studies. Contributors review the challenges of conducting a salary-equity study for nonfaculty administrators and staff—who constitute the majority of employees, even in academic institutions—and examine the advantages and disadvantages of using hierarchical linear modeling to measure pay equity. They present a case-study approach to illustrate the political and practical challenges that researchers often face when conducting a salary-equity study for an institution. This is a companion volume to *Conducting Salary-Equity Studies: Alternative Approaches to Research* (IR115).
ISBN: 0-7879-6863-3

IR116    **Reporting Higher Education Results: Missing Links in the Performance Chain**
*Joseph C. Burke, Henrick P. Minassians*
The authors review performance reporting's coverage, content, and customers, they examine in depth the reporting indicators, types, and policy concerns, and they compare them among different states' reports. They highlight weaknesses in our current performance reporting—such as a lack of comparable indicators for assessing the quality of undergraduate education— and make recommendations about how to best use and improve performance information.
ISBN: 0-7879-6336-4

IR115    **Conducting Salary-Equity Studies: Alternative Approaches to Research**
*Robert K. Toutkoushian*
Synthesizing nearly 30 years of research on salary equity from the field of economics and the experiences of past studies, this issue launches an important dialogue between scholars and institutional researchers on the methodology and application of salary-equity studies in today's higher education institutions. The first of a two-volume set on the subject, it also bridges the gap between academic research and the more pragmatic statistical and political considerations in real-life institutional salary studies.
ISBN: 0-7879-6335-6

IR114    **Evaluating Faculty Performance**
*Carol L. Colbeck*
This issue brings new insights to faculty work and its assessment in light of
reconsideration of faculty work roles, rapid technological change, increasing
bureaucratization of the core work of higher education, and public
accountability for performance. Exploring successful methods that individuals,
institutions, and promotion and tenure committees are using for evaluations of
faculty performance for career development, this issue is an indispensable
guide to academic administrators and institutional researchers involved in the
faculty evaluation process.
ISBN: 0-7879-6334-8

IR113    **Knowledge Management: Building a Competitive Advantage in Higher
Education**
*Andreea M. Serban, Jing Luan*
Provides a comprehensive discussion of knowledge management, covering its
theoretical, practical, and technological aspects with an emphasis on their
relevance for applications in institutional research. Chapters examine the
theoretical basis and impact of data mining; discuss the role of institutional
research in customer relationship management; and provide a framework for
the integration of institutional research within the larger context of organization
learning. With a synopsis of technologies that support knowledge management
and an exploration of future developments in this field, this volume assists
institutional researchers and analysts in taking advantage of the opportunities
of knowledge management and addressing its challenges.
ISBN: 0-7879-6291-0

IR112    **Balancing Qualitative and Quantitative Information for Effective Decision
Support**
*Richard D. Howard, Kenneth W. Borland Jr.*
Establishes methods for integration of numeric data and its contextual
application. With theoretical and practical examples, contributors explore the
techniques and realities of creating, communicating, and using balanced
decision support information. Chapters discuss the critical role of measurement
in building institutional quality; examples of conceptual and theoretical
frameworks and their application for the creation of evaluation information;
and methods of communicating data and information in relation to its decision
support function.
ISBN: 0-7879-5796-8

IR111    **Higher Education as Competitive Enterprise: When Markets Matter**
*Robert Zemsky, Susan Shaman, Daniel B. Shapiro*
Offers a comprehensive history of the development and implementation of
Collegiate Results Instrument (CRI), a tool for mapping the connection between
market forces and educational outcomes in higher education. Chapters detail
the methods that CRI uses to help institutions to remain value centered by
becoming market smart.
ISBN: 0-7879-5795-X

IR110    **Measuring What Matters: Competency-Based Learning Models in Higher
Education**
*Richard Voorhees*
An analysis of the findings of the National Postsecondary Education Cooperative
project on data and policy implications of national skill standards, this issue
provides researchers, faculty, and academic administrators with the tools needed
to deal effectively with the emerging competency-based initiatives.
ISBN: 0-7879-1411-8

# NEW DIRECTIONS FOR INSTITUTIONAL RESEARCH

# ORDER FORM SUBSCRIPTION AND SINGLE ISSUES

## DISCOUNTED BACK ISSUES:

Use this form to receive 20% off all back issues of *New Directions for Institutional Research*.
All single issues priced at **$23.20** (normally $29.00)

| TITLE | ISSUE NO. | ISBN |
|-------|-----------|------|
| _____ | _____ | _____ |
| _____ | _____ | _____ |
| _____ | _____ | _____ |

*Call 888-378-2537 or see mailing instructions below. When calling, mention the promotional code JB9ND
to receive your discount. For a complete list of issues, please visit www.josseybass.com/go/ndir*

## SUBSCRIPTIONS: (1 YEAR, 4 ISSUES)

☐ New Order    ☐ Renewal

|  | | |
|---|---|---|
| U.S. | ☐ Individual: $100 | ☐ Institutional: $249 |
| CANADA/MEXICO | ☐ Individual: $100 | ☐ Institutional: $289 |
| ALL OTHERS | ☐ Individual: $124 | ☐ Institutional: $323 |

*Call 888-378-2537 or see mailing and pricing instructions below.
Online subscriptions are available at www.interscience.wiley.com*

## ORDER TOTALS:

Issue / Subscription Amount: $ _____

Shipping Amount: $ _____
*(for single issues only – subscription prices include shipping)*

**Total Amount:** $ _____

| SHIPPING CHARGES: | |
|---|---|
| First Item | $5.00 |
| Each Add'l Item | $3.00 |

*(No sales tax for U.S. subscriptions. Canadian residents, add GST for subscription orders. Individual rate subscriptions must
be paid by personal check or credit card. Individual rate subscriptions may not be resold as library copies.)*

## BILLING & SHIPPING INFORMATION:

☐ **PAYMENT ENCLOSED:** *(U.S. check or money order only. All payments must be in U.S. dollars.)*

☐ **CREDIT CARD:** ☐ VISA  ☐ MC  ☐ AMEX

Card number _____ Exp. Date _____

Card Holder Name _____ Card Issue # _____

Signature _____ Day Phone _____

☐ **BILL ME:** *(U.S. institutional orders only. Purchase order required.)*

Purchase order # _____
Federal Tax ID 13559302 • GST 89102-8052

Name _____

Address _____

Phone _____ E-mail _____

Copy or detach page and send to:    **John Wiley & Sons, PTSC, 5th Floor
989 Market Street, San Francisco, CA 94103-1741**

Order Form can also be faxed to:    **888-481-2665**

PROMO JB9ND